Baking Happiness

Delicious, Colorful *Desserts*
to Brighten Every Day

Rosie Madaschi

Creator of Sugar & Salt Cookies

PAGE STREET
PUBLISHING CO.

PAGE STREET
PUBLISHING CO.

First published in 2020 by
Page Street Publishing Co.
27 Congress Street, Suite 105
Salem, MA 01970
www.pagestreetpublishing.com

Distributed by Macmillan, sales in Canada by The Canadian Manda Group.

24   23   22   21   20   1   2   3   4   5

ISBN-13: 978-1-64567-138-1
ISBN-10: 1-64567-138-0

Library of Congress Control Number: 2019957307

Cover and book design by Kylie Alexander for Page Street Publishing Co.
Photography by Rosie Madaschi and Leah de Sousa

Printed and bound in the United States

Dedication

To my son, Sebastian—my best buddy, biggest supporter
and number-one fan

Welcome to the Sweet Life

Hi bakers! Welcome to my first ever cookbook. If you've been following my baking journey on Instagram, then you already know you're in for a sweet treat. To those of you who are new to my world, let me tell you a bit about me and what you're going to find in this book.

My name is Rosie and I am the pink- and sprinkle-obsessed person behind Sugar & Salt Cookies, my little business specializing in cakes and sweet treats in all the colors of the rainbow. When I began baking, bright and bold colors weren't used much by other bakers. Pastels were the more popular choice. I like to think of myself as a bit of an ambassador for brightly colored cakes and desserts. I hope you have your food coloring ready!

Never in my wildest dreams did I think I would end up a cake decorator. I've always loved eating cakes and sweets (just ask my dentist) but only if they involved absolutely no effort on my part. My interest was just the eating. Period. My other great love was (and still is) history. How these two loves led me to where I am today is an interesting story.

In 2012 my first child was born, a beautiful boy named Sebastian. When he was only a few months old, I was surprised with our first family holiday—a trip to Paris. French history was of particular interest to me, so to say I was excited is an understatement. The whole experience was magical, including my first trip to the famous Ladurée patisserie. I was utterly blown away by the array of such perfectly presented treats and torn between wanting to admire their beauty or devour them. They looked way too pretty to eat, each one a perfect work of art. Well I did eat as many as was physically possible, but not before taking about 100 photos. Being in Paris, surrounded by the magnificent history, culture, beauty and edible art, set my heart on fire.

Over the next few years, I dedicated a lot of time to baking (and baked my second child, beautiful Lily). I am self-taught, so this involved a lot of online tutorials, reading, etc. It also involved a LOT of trial and error. There eventually came a time when I felt confident enough to turn it into a profession, so that's exactly what I did. At this point it was only going to be a short-term gig though. My plan was to go back to university once both my children were in school, to study writing so that I could write history books for children. Things often don't turn out as planned though, right? Fast-forward a few years and here I am. Still no writing degree, but writing a book anyway. Not a history book, but something that I love equally. I'd say things turned out even better than planned.

I once read *Like Water for Chocolate*, where the main character expressed herself through cooking. This idea stayed with me for a long time and largely inspired some of my cake and dessert designs. I should mention here that I am NOT a good cook. People will often tell my son what a fantastic cook I am, and his response is always the same: "My mum is an amazing baker, but just an okay cook." There's a difference, people! Baking has been an incredible outlet for me in good times and bad. Ultimately, I think that's how a baker finds their decorating style. My style has evolved over time, but one thing has remained —baking makes me happy and that happiness is always reflected in what I create.

How does baking make me happy, you ask? For starters, there's a batch of cupcakes ready to be eaten pretty much 24/7 in my house. No further explanation required. But mostly, it's about the process. I begin by finding inspiration. It could be a feeling, something I see, something I hear. Inspiration is all around us, everywhere we go. It's just a matter of finding it and using it for something else; in my case, baking. Once I find my inspiration, I begin to envision what I'm going to make, how it will look and how it will taste. This is where my creativity comes into play. Then I go through the steps of bringing this vision to life, and that is where my happiness lies. This happiness hasn't always come from succeeding the first time though. I've had many failures. Sometimes happiness comes from looking back to when I began, realizing how far I've come and being grateful that I never gave up.

In this book, each chapter is divided into two sections: recipes and decorating tutorials. The recipes have been carefully crafted to remain simple, but also delicious, and the tutorials are full of my fun and bright signature designs, as well as some classic favorites. You'll begin each chapter by baking. Be sure to reference my advice regarding equipment, temperature and ingredients (page 9). The success of your baked goods will determine the outcome of the next step, which is decorating. For example, lining your cake pans and leveling your cakes correctly will result in even layers with smooth sides, which is crucial in order to execute my method of stacking and frosting a cake. My aim is to teach you how to re-create my designs and become familiar with the methods I use, from the beginning of the baking process all the way to the storage information and everything in between.

My hope is that you can use what you learn to tap into your own creativity and find your unique style: to experiment, make mistakes, learn from them and find out which process brings you the most happiness. The main thing is that you have fun along the way. For me, the ultimate goal of baking is a balance of making something that tastes and looks good, and this is what I offer you. Homer Simpson was right when he said, "You don't win friends with salad." Well, with cake you do. Everyone loves cake. I hope you will love mine.

Enjoy,

Rosie x

Rosie Alladaselli

Baking 101

I know you're super excited to get started, but before you begin, I need to lay down some ground rules. Baking is not like cooking. In cooking, there is much more room to improvise and make mistakes. I would know, because I'm a terrible cook and have had some of the world's worst fails, yet always manage to come out of them with a family full of satisfied bellies. Baked goods are not as forgiving. There is a science to them, therefore it is crucial to have the proper equipment and follow recipes carefully. To give you an example, let's look at salt. In most of these recipes you will find only about a teaspoon of it, so someone may think it can be left out. What could a teaspoon possibly change? Salt is magic though; a tiny amount enhances flavor like you wouldn't believe. Without it, an entire cake can taste quite bland. This is how I came up with my business name, Sugar & Salt Cookies. Sugar is the ingredient I use the most of and salt the least. But they are both equally important when baking.

TOOLS

Aside from general baking equipment such as bowls and whisks, this is what you will need to execute the recipes and tutorials in this book:

- 3 (6 x 3–inch [15 x 7.5–cm]) round cake pans
- 9 x 13–inch (23 x 33–cm) rectangular cake pans
- Stand mixer
- Digital kitchen scale
- Oven thermometer
- Candy thermometer
- Cake decorating turntable
- Piping bags
- Piping tips: 1A, 1M, 8B, 21, 32 and 199 (I use Wilton)
- Angled offset metal spatulas in various sizes
- 10-inch (25.5-cm) cake boards, minimum 4 mm thick
- Rolling pin
- Medium spring action ice cream scoop
- Paintbrushes
- Cookie cutters
- Cake leveler
- Large cake scraper
- Regular cupcake pan
- 12-hole nonstick donut pan, 3-inch (7.5-cm) cavities
- Nonstick 9-inch (23-cm) round tart pan

I strongly recommend using a digital kitchen scale to measure all ingredients. It does not need to be an expensive top-of-the-line scale; there are many inexpensive ones that work perfectly. Measuring by volume is nowhere near as accurate, and a small change can significantly alter a recipe. All of the ingredients in this book, including liquids, have been written with the weight in grams for complete precision.

TEMPERATURE

The baking times and temperatures in these recipes are for conventional ovens. Oven temperature is everything. An oven's built-in thermometer is not accurate enough. You should use a separate oven thermometer and hang it on the middle rack for the most accurate reading. Oven thermometers are inexpensive and will make all the difference to the outcome of your baked goods. Even a difference of a few degrees can potentially ruin a recipe. You don't want to end up with a cake that collapses from underbaking or is dry from overbaking. The oven door shouldn't be opened throughout the baking time unless stated otherwise, as it may affect the temperature. It is also important to follow my instructions on which rack to bake on. Some recipes bake quite tall, so they must be baked on a lower rack.

I mostly use low oven temperatures for the recipes in this book for the following reasons:

- With cakes, it ensures an even rise and bake. If the temperature is too high, the outside will bake much quicker than the inside. This is especially the case when using deep pans like I do for the cakes here.

- With colored baked goods, it ensures the colors remain vibrant without browning.

Ingredients should be room temperature, unless stated otherwise. I swear I'm not just being a pain for the sake of it. I really want your baked goods to be perfect. Cold ingredients do not emulsify well and will impact the outcome. Every room will be a different temperature, but a rough guideline is to let cold ingredients sit at room temperature for about an hour before using them.

The temperature of the butter used in each recipe throughout this book is of particular importance and will have the most impact on the final outcome. The three main temperatures are:

- Softened. The butter will be solid, but soft enough to spread or beat in a stand mixer. It should not be warm, greasy or shiny.
- Partially melted. The butter will be half liquid and half solid. This is achieved by heating cold butter in the microwave for approximately 30 seconds at first, then in 10-second increments until half melted.
- Melted and cooled. The butter is completely liquid with no solid chunks. Allow it to cool until it is no longer hot, but do not allow it to solidify. Approximately 5 minutes is sufficient cooling time.

COLOR

It is very important that you do not use liquid food coloring in any of these recipes. Gel only! For the most vibrant colors, I use the AmeriColor electric range or the Chefmaster neon range. If you use regular gel colors (e.g., pink instead of electric/neon pink), then the final color will be quite soft, not bright and vibrant. The amounts used in my recipes are just a guideline. You can add more or less depending on how bright you want your color. If you want a brighter color, make sure to add one drop at a time and combine well before adding more.

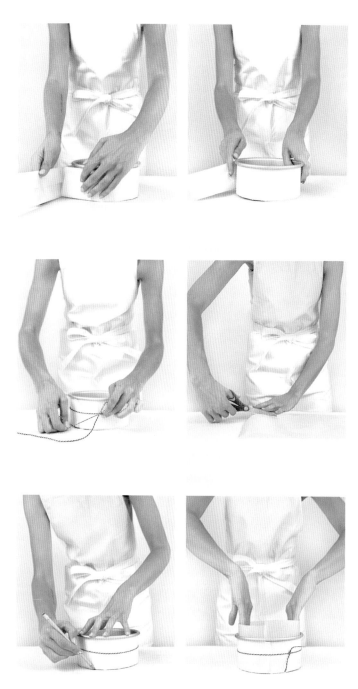

LINING CAKE PANS

Lining cake pans correctly is crucial to the outcome. Not only does it help to release the cake from the pan without getting stuck, but it also helps with an even rise and bake. With all cakes, the outside is always the first part to bake. With deep cake pans that hold a lot of batter, it is especially important that the outsides and tops don't set too quickly. I use a low temperature to help this process. I also line the outside of the pan, as this prevents it from heating up too much and baking the sides too quickly. Just follow these steps to line your pan:

1. Roll out a sheet of parchment paper long enough to wrap around the pan twice. For a 6-inch (15-cm) round pan, this will be 38 inches (96 cm).

2. Lay the paper flat and then fold it upwards 3 inches (7.5 cm). Continue folding it over until there is no paper left to fold. It will be the same height as the pan.

3. Wrap it around the pan and secure by tying some twine around it. Repeat with the other two pans.

4. To line the insides, roll out two sheets of parchment paper that are each 19 inches (48 cm) long. From the first sheet, cut a strip along the bottom approximately 4 inches (10 cm) in height and then another at the top. Discard the middle section.

5. With the second sheet, cut the same strip at the bottom, but with the top section, trace the cake pan three times. Cut out each circle and set aside. You will have three strips that are 19 inches (48 cm) long and 4 inches (10 cm) high and three circles that are 6 inches (15 cm) in diameter.

6. Spray each pan with nonstick cooking spray and place a long strip along the inside of each with the straight part facing down (the line where you cut will be slightly uneven, so this part will face up). Lastly, place a cut-out circle on the bottom of each pan and use your fingers to press it into the sides.

CAKE LEVELING

Cakes should always be chilled before leveling. I know it's tempting to level a cake as soon as it's cooled and eat the scraps. Trust me, I've been there. More than once. It's not enough for the cake to be cooled though, it really needs to be chilled. If you don't chill the cake sufficiently, you'll end up with a crumbly mess. Just follow these steps for a perfectly leveled cake:

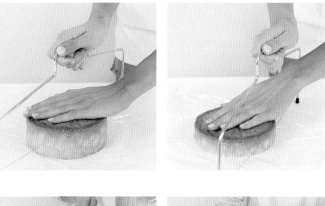

1. Once the cake has been chilled overnight, remove it from the plastic wrap and place it on a clean, smooth surface, such as a kitchen counter.

2. Adjust the wire on the cake leveler so it sits right in the middle of the cake. Holding the cake in place with one hand, use your other hand to slide the leveler back and forth so it cuts through the middle of the cake.

3. Remove the top layer and place it on your surface, then repeat the process to cut off the top domed part of the cake. Eat this immediately. Wrap the layers and chill them until you are ready to frost your cake.

CUTTING A CAKE

Tall cakes seem to intimidate a lot of people when it comes to cutting them. Fear not, the solution is quite simple. All you need is a cutting board and a big knife!

1. Hold the cutting board next to the cake, about 2 inches (5 cm) from the edge. Use the knife to slice all the way through the cake.

2. Push the slice onto the cutting board and then lay it flat.

3. Depending on how large you want the slices, cut the slab into pieces and serve.

BAKING BLUNDERS

Some days, things just go wrong. It happens to the best of us. These problems often come down to not following recipes properly, accidently forgetting or adding too much of an ingredient, incorrect oven temperature or having bad karma. Just kidding. (Although I could swear at times that the cake gods are out to get me.) I've had days where absolutely everything has gone wrong, and I've been baking full time for years! So if it happens to you, don't beat yourself up. The weather plays a massive part in baking too. Most of the time when things don't work for me, it's in the middle of summer or winter. It's even worse if it's particularly humid where you live, so factor that in, especially when working with things like buttercream and chocolate. Below are a few common issues that people often encounter, most of which are avoidable if using an oven thermometer and digital kitchen scale.

CAKE RISES TOO MUCH IN THE MIDDLE

The cakes in this book will be slightly domed as they are baked in deep pans. If the center of the cake is significantly higher than the sides, however, these are some possible reasons:

- The oven temperature may be too high, resulting in the sides baking and setting too quickly. When this happens, the cake has nowhere left to rise but in the center.
- You may have added too much flour, which makes the structure of the cake too strong. When this happens, it prevents the leavening agent gases from escaping until they finally erupt through the center.
- You may have overmixed your batter. This causes gluten formation, which makes more air bubbles. These bubbles make the cake rise rapidly, and if the sides of the cake have already set, the bubbles have nowhere to rise except in the center.

CAKE SINKS

- You may have added too much leavening agent. When this happens, the cake rises rapidly, but if the structure is weak, it collapses once it's removed from the heat.
- The oven temperature may be too low or the cake hasn't baked long enough, resulting in it not baking the whole way through and collapsing once it's removed from the oven.
- You may have overmixed your batter. This causes gluten formation, which makes more air bubbles. These bubbles make the cake rise rapidly, but if the structure is weak, it collapses once removed from the heat.

CUPCAKES OVERFLOW FROM THE LINERS

- You may have overfilled them. If you fill the liners more than the recipe states, the batter will rise and not set in time, resulting in it spilling over the sides.
- You may have overmixed your batter. This causes gluten formation, which makes more air bubbles. These bubbles make the cupcakes rise more rapidly, and potentially spill over the sides if they haven't begun to set yet.

CUPCAKE LINERS PEEL AWAY FROM THE CUPCAKES

- The cupcakes may be underbaked. When this happens, the cupcakes shrink as they cool, resulting in the liners pulling away.
- You may have stored the cupcakes before they had completely cooled, locking in any residual heat. The moisture from this heat can cause the liners to pull away from the cupcakes.
- You may have left the cupcakes to cool in the pan, which will allow a build up of moisture around the liners, resulting in them pulling away.

- More often than not, it's because the oven temperature is too low. When this happens, the cookies don't set quickly enough, allowing the butter to melt and spread.
- You may have creamed the butter and sugar too long. When this happens, too much air is incorporated, which causes cookies to spread.
- You may not have chilled the dough for the correct amount of time as per the recipe instructions.

CHOCOLATE DOESN'T SET

- You may have overheated the chocolate. Unfortunately, when this happens, the chocolate can't be saved. Make sure to melt chocolate in small increments and stir after every addition.
- There may be humidity, which prevents chocolate from setting. Try placing what you have made in the fridge for 1 to 2 minutes (no longer, or it will absorb moisture).

CHOCOLATE SEIZES

- It may have come in contact with water, so always use oil-based colors and make sure bowls and other utensils are completely clean and dry.
- It may have been exposed to something too cold. Always avoid surfaces and utensils that are cold such as stone or stainless-steel countertops.

STORAGE

I'll be surprised if anything you make lasts longer than a day, but just in case, here is some information on storage.

- Frosted cakes need to be refrigerated. Bring a cake to room temperature before cutting and eating, as it will be quite hard straight out of the fridge. Depending on the temperature of your room, this can take between 30 minutes to 2 hours. If you take a cake out too early and the buttercream becomes too soft, just pop it back in the fridge for another 15 minutes. Cakes are best served at room temperature as the buttercream will be smooth and the cake layers soft and tender. Once it's been cut, store it in an airtight container in the fridge. The airtight container will keep it from drying out. Consume within five days.
- Frosted cupcakes can be left in a cake/cupcake box at room temperature for up to three days. It is generally recommended to not store them in airtight tupperware.
- All cookies can be left in an airtight container at room temperature for up to two weeks, although they are fresher the first week.
- Cake cones, cake pops, cakesicles, tarts, donuts and cookie sandwiches need to be stored in an airtight container in the fridge. They do not need to come to room temperature before consuming. Consume within five days.
- All of the cakes in this book can be stored in the freezer prior to decorating for up to two months. Wrap each completely cooled cake twice in plastic wrap and then once with aluminum foil.

Cakeaholics

Whenever I'm organizing a celebration, the cake is always at the top of the to-do list. Cake is the life of every party. I have been to parties that I wasn't actually interested in attending simply because I knew there would be good cake. You know that quote "I'm just here for cake"? Well obviously I'm not the only one. That quote is printed on posters and T-shirts and coffee mugs. It is a way of life. Better than eating cake is making it yourself first. There's so much more satisfaction in it. Plus, when you know how to bake good cakes, everyone loves you just a little bit more. It's a win-win.

The cake recipes in this chapter make tall cakes. The cakes are stable enough to support the weight and height of the stacked layers but are also moist and full of flavor. They have also been designed to have smooth sides, which means no crumb coating (you're welcome). The absolute kicker, though, is that they require no creaming—so no stand mixer! Just quick, easy and delicious recipes.

For me, the number one indicator of a good cake is when it tastes amazing on its own without buttercream. Too often, overly sweet buttercream is used to compensate for a bland or dry cake. None of that here! In fact, my kids only eat my cakes plain these days. They love my buttercream, but it usually ends up all over their clothes and my furniture, so I avoid it when I can. No complaints at all. In fact, I often find them deep in cake conversation, discussing the moistness and texture and flavor. I have unintentionally turned them into miniature cake snobs and critics. They are not the kind of children you want at your party, because they will not hesitate to tell you if your cake is no good. On top of that, they will then walk around the room telling everyone that their mum makes the best cakes in the world. I don't condone this, but it's sort of cute how loyal they are.

My decorating tutorials are designed to teach you exactly how I create some of my most popular or favorite designs, down to the very last detail. Once you've mastered my tutorials, you'll be able to mix and match the recipes, colors and decorating methods to suit your personal preference or style. The options are endless!

Vanilla Cake (page 19)

Chocolate Cake (page 20)

Lemon Cake (page 21)

Vanilla Cake

In a baker's world, I believe you're only as good as your vanilla cake. Yet the perfect recipe seems to elude so many. Everyone has different expectations of the vanilla cake, and the poor thing just can't keep up sometimes. I have personally spent more time on this recipe than any other in an attempt to tick all the boxes and keep everyone happy. I have also nearly ended up in a vanilla-cake coma from overconsumption of all the test recipes, just to get it right. I love this recipe so much that I use it as the base for a few other recipes too. I hope it brings you as much happiness as it has brought me, my family, my neighbors, my clients and all the random people who come knocking on my front door because the sweet vanilla smell has lured them there like a cake Pied Piper. (I'm kidding, but I have had people not leave my house because they've loved the smell so much.)

Makes three 6-inch (15-cm) round cakes

4 cups (500 g) all-purpose flour

1 tbsp (12 g) baking powder

¾ tsp baking soda

1½ tsp (4 g) salt

1¾ cups (393 g) unsalted butter, partially melted

3 cups (600 g) sugar

4 large eggs, plus 2 egg yolks

1 cup (240 g) full fat milk

1 cup (240 g) full fat Greek yogurt

¼ cup (60 g) vegetable oil

2 tbsp (30 g) vanilla extract

Preheat the oven to 320°F (160°C), and line three cake pans using the method on page 12.

In a large bowl, whisk together the flour, baking powder, baking soda and salt. In another large bowl, whisk together the butter and sugar until combined. Add the eggs one at a time, whisking until incorporated before adding the next. Add the egg yolks, milk, yogurt, oil and vanilla extract and whisk again to combine. Pour the wet ingredients into the dry ingredients and whisk until just combined, occasionally scraping the botton of the bowl to break up any clumps of flour. Do not overmix.

Pour the batter evenly into the cake pans. There will be approximately 700 grams of batter per pan. Place the pans in the oven on the rack one below the middle and bake for 75 minutes. To test for doneness, stick a skewer in the cake. If it comes out with some soft crumbs, then it's perfect, as the cakes will continue to bake a little once removed from the oven.

Allow the cakes to cool for 15 minutes before removing them from the pans and placing them on a wire rack. Once cooled completely, wrap each cake twice with plastic wrap and place them in the fridge overnight before decorating.

Chocolate Cake

The chocolate cake—my nemesis. If it were possible for a cake to play mind games with you, then this one is the main culprit. Just when I'd think I'd nailed it and would begin to ascend my throne as a cake queen, something would bring me back down to reality. Too rich, too airy, too chocolatey, not chocolatey enough. Just be perfect already so that I can put an end to the cocoa, which seems to spread to every inch of my kitchen when I pour it out. The problem is that there are too many options in a chocolate cake recipe. Oil or butter? Coffee or no coffee? Real chocolate or no real chocolate? Buttermilk or regular milk? It's the cake equivalent of Einstein's special relativity equation. OKAY. I might be exaggerating, but it gives you an idea of my frustration. After seven trials, I finally settled on my perfect recipe—and then made it another four times just to be sure. It's rich without being heavy. Not so light that it's like eating air, but not dense either. The chocolate flavor is spot-on, thanks to the magic of the coffee. And no, you can't taste the coffee at all. This is definitely the one.

Makes three 6-inch (15-cm) round cakes ·

3 cups (375 g) all-purpose flour

1¼ cups (125 g) unsweetened cocoa powder

3 cups (600 g) sugar

1 tbsp (12 g) baking powder

1 tsp baking soda

1½ tsp (4 g) salt

1 cup (227 g) unsalted butter, partially melted

4 large eggs

1½ cups (360 g) buttermilk

½ cup (120 g) vegetable oil

1 tbsp (15 g) vanilla extract

½ cup (120 g) hot water

1 tbsp (6 g) instant coffee granules

Preheat the oven to 320°F (160°C) and line three cake pans using the method on page 12.

In a large bowl, whisk together the flour, cocoa powder, sugar, baking powder, baking soda and salt. In another large bowl, whisk together the butter, eggs, buttermilk, oil and vanilla extract until combined. Pour the hot water and coffee in a glass and stir to combine. Set aside. Pour the wet ingredients into the dry ingredients. As you're whisking the wet and dry ingredients together, slowly add the hot coffee and continue to whisk until just combined, occasionally scraping the bottom of the bowl to break up any clumps of flour. Do not overmix.

Pour the batter evenly into the cake pans. There will be approximately 700 grams of batter per pan. Place the pans in the oven on the rack one below the middle and bake for 70 minutes. To test for doneness, stick a skewer in the cake. If it comes out with some soft crumbs, then it's perfect, as the cakes will continue to bake a little once removed from the oven.

Allow the cakes to cool for 15 minutes before removing them from the pans and placing them on a wire rack. Once cooled completely, wrap each cake twice with plastic wrap and place them in the fridge overnight before decorating.

Lemon Cake

If you don't like lemon cake—yes, these people exist and walk among us—then it's likely you haven't had a good one. Lemons are naturally sour, so it can be tricky using them to make something sweet. It's all about balance and the right quantities. When flavoring a cake, nothing works better than natural ingredients. With lemons, you get two ingredients for the price of one. The zest is the yellow part of the peel. I repeat, the yellow part. Do not use the white part unless you want people spitting out your cake. The yellow zest is full of oils that give that pure lemon flavor. The lemon's juice is acidic, giving that citrusy, zesty kick. I use both lemon zest and juice in this recipe, then top it off with some lemon extract to enhance the flavor even more, just 'cause I like being a little extra sometimes.

Makes three 6-inch (15-cm) round cakes ···

4 cups (500 g) all-purpose flour

1 tbsp (12 g) baking powder

¾ tsp baking soda

1½ tsp (4 g) salt

1¾ cups (393 g) unsalted butter, partially melted

3 cups (600 g) sugar

Zest of 1 medium lemon

4 large eggs, plus 2 egg yolks

1 cup (240 g) full fat milk

1 cup (240 g) full fat Greek yogurt

¼ cup (60 g) vegetable oil

1 tbsp (15 g) lemon juice

1 tbsp (15 g) lemon extract

Preheat the oven to 320°F (160°C) and line three cake pans using the method on page 12.

In a large bowl, whisk together the flour, baking powder, baking soda and salt. In another large bowl, whisk together the butter, sugar and lemon zest until combined. Add the eggs one at a time, whisking until incorporated before adding the next. Add the egg yolks, milk, yogurt, oil, lemon juice and lemon extract and whisk again to combine. Pour the wet ingredients into the dry ingredients and whisk until just combined, occasionally scraping the bottom of the bowl to break up any clumps of flour. Do not overmix.

Pour the batter evenly into the cake pans. There will be approximately 700 grams of batter per pan. Place the pans in the oven on the rack one below the middle and bake for 75 minutes. To test for doneness, stick a skewer in the cake. If it comes out with some soft crumbs, then it's perfect, as the cakes will continue to bake a little once removed from the oven.

Allow the cakes to cool for 15 minutes before removing them from the pans and placing them on a wire rack. Once cooled completely, wrap each cake twice with plastic wrap and place them in the fridge overnight before decorating.

Caramel Cake (page 25)

Coconut Cake (page 24)

Pink Lemonade Cake (page 23)

Pink Lemonade Cake

There are a few stories going around about the origins of pink lemonade and what it actually tastes like. Some say it's just colored lemonade. Others say it's lemonade mixed with raspberry or strawberry juice. From my research, it would appear the most common theory is that it's an even sweeter version of regular lemonade and colored pink. Well, how to turn this into a cake flavor? I started with lemon extract as my base. Then I experimented with raspberry and strawberry flavoring. They were both nice. Suddenly it hit me—if pink lemonade is a sweeter version of regular lemonade, I just need more sugar. The answer—cotton candy flavoring! Cotton candy is just spun sugar, so if you add it to something else, it's going to enhance the sweetness. Bingo!

Makes three 6-inch (15-cm) round cakes ··

4 cups (500 g) all-purpose flour

1 tbsp (12 g) baking powder

¾ tsp baking soda

1½ tsp (4 g) salt

1¾ cups (393 g) unsalted butter, partially melted

3 cups (600 g) sugar

4 large eggs, plus 2 egg yolks

1 cup (240 g) full fat milk

1 cup (240 g) full fat Greek yogurt

¼ cup (60 g) vegetable oil

1 tbsp (15 g) lemon extract

½ tbsp (7.5 g) cotton candy flavoring

Electric/neon pink gel food coloring

Preheat the oven to 320°F (160°C) and line the cake pans using the method on page 12.

In a large bowl, whisk together the flour, baking powder, baking soda and salt. In another large bowl, whisk together the butter and sugar until combined. Add the eggs one at a time, whisking until incorporated before adding the next. Add the egg yolks, milk, yogurt, oil, lemon extract, cotton candy flavoring and 3 to 4 drops of pink gel coloring and whisk again to combine. Pour the wet ingredients into the dry ingredients and whisk until just combined, occasionally scraping the bottom of the bowl to break up any clumps of flour. Do not overmix.

Pour the batter evenly into the cake pans. There will be approximately 700 grams of batter per pan. Place the pans in the oven on the rack one below the middle and bake for 75 minutes. To test for doneness, stick a skewer in the cake. If it comes out with some soft crumbs, then it's perfect, as the cakes will continue to bake a little once removed from the oven.

Allow the cakes to cool for 15 minutes before removing them from the pans and placing them on a wire rack. Once cooled completely, wrap each cake twice with plastic wrap and place them in the fridge overnight before decorating.

Coconut Cake

Every year my birthday cake is coconut. I just can't go past it. I have a bit of an obsessive personality —if you hadn't already come to that conclusion—so when I find something I love, I stick with it. This is especially evident when you visit my house. I eat coconut-flavored yogurt, use coconut-scented moisturizer, have coconut-scented candles. I even use coconut-scented air fresheners. That's love right there. For me this cake is extra special because the shredded coconut gives it a slightly different texture. The coconut doesn't dissolve, so you can feel and taste those little shredded bits while you're chewing. It's just sooo good.

Makes three 6-inch (15-cm) round cakes ···

4 cups (500 g) all-purpose flour

1 tbsp (12 g) baking powder

¾ tsp baking soda

1½ tsp (4 g) salt

1¾ cups (393 g) unsalted butter, partially melted

3 cups (600 g) sugar

1½ cups (120 g) shredded coconut

4 large eggs, plus 2 egg yolks

1 cup (240 g) full fat canned coconut milk, room temperature

1 cup (240 g) full fat Greek yogurt

¼ cup (60 g) vegetable oil

4 tsp (20 g) coconut extract

Preheat the oven to 320°F (160°C) and line three cake pans using the method on page 12.

In a large bowl, whisk together the flour, baking powder, baking soda and salt. In another large bowl, whisk together the butter, sugar and shredded coconut until combined. Add the eggs, one at a time, whisking until incorporated before adding the next. Add the egg yolks, coconut milk, yogurt, oil and coconut extract and whisk again to combine. Pour the wet ingredients into the dry ingredients and whisk until just combined, occasionally scraping the bottom of the bowl to break up any clumps of flour. Do not overmix.

Pour the batter evenly into the cake pans. There will be approximately 720 grams of batter per pan. Place the pans in the oven on the rack one below the middle and bake for 75 minutes. To test for doneness, stick a skewer in the cake. If it comes out with some soft crumbs, then it's perfect, as the cakes will continue to bake a little once removed from the oven.

Allow the cakes to cool for 15 minutes before removing them from the pans and placing on a wire rack. Once cooled completely, wrap each cake twice with plastic wrap and place them in the fridge overnight before decorating.

Caramel Cake

Unsatisfied with caramel cake recipes that were essentially a vanilla cake with caramel filling, I began my mission to develop an actual caramel-flavored cake. This one tested my patience more than any other, but when I finally nailed it, I celebrated for about three days (by eating all the cake that had built up in my kitchen). Brown sugar was the first step. It was good, but it could have been better. Then came the white chocolate. Life changing! It enhanced the caramel flavor like you wouldn't believe. My mum, who has amazing willpower when it comes to eating desserts (clearly I didn't take after her), just couldn't stop eating it. Well, she did long enough to tell me how delicious it was, but then resumed her face stuffing. I can't be 100 percent sure, but I think I even saw her eyes roll back into her head at one point. Just saying.

Makes three 6-inch (15-cm) round cakes ···

4 cups (500 g) all-purpose flour

1 tbsp (12 g) baking powder

¾ tsp baking soda

1½ tsp (4 g) salt

1⅔ cups (280 g) white chocolate, melted and cooled

1½ cups (340 g) unsalted butter, partially melted

2¼ cups (450 g) light brown sugar, packed

4 large eggs, plus 2 egg yolks

1 cup (240 g) full fat milk

1 cup (240 g) full fat Greek yogurt

¼ cup (60 g) vegetable oil

4 tsp (20 g) vanilla extract

Preheat the oven to 320°F (160°C) and line the cake pans using the method on page 12.

In a large bowl, whisk together the flour, baking powder, baking soda and salt. In another large bowl, whisk together the melted chocolate, butter and sugar until combined. Add the eggs one at a time, whisking until incorporated before adding the next. Add the egg yolks, milk, yogurt, oil and vanilla extract and whisk again to combine. Pour the wet ingredients into the dry ingredients and whisk until just combined, occasionally scraping the bottom of the bowl to break up any clumps of flour. Do not overmix.

Pour the batter evenly into three cake pans. There will be approximately 720 grams of batter per pan. Place the pans in the oven on the rack one below the middle and bake for 75 minutes. To test for doneness, stick a skewer in the cake. If it comes out with some soft crumbs, then it's perfect, as the cakes will continue to bake a little once removed from the oven.

Allow the cakes to cool for 15 minutes before removing them from the pans and placing them on a wire rack. Once cooled completely, wrap each cake twice with plastic wrap and place them in the fridge overnight before decorating.

Signature Buttercream

If you've never made a meringue-based buttercream, you have no idea what you've been missing. Aside from tasting heavenly (seriously, you can eat it like ice cream), it is also an absolute dream to work with. It's soft and silky, making it very easy to achieve smooth sides on a cake. To date I have experimented with Swiss, Italian and French and loved them all. I used Swiss for a long time, but then was introduced to French and never looked back. French buttercream is made with either egg yolks or whole eggs, making it extra rich and creamy. While I loved this, I often found it difficult to achieve bright colors, as the yolks give the buttercream a yellow tinge. In came the Italian! Italian meringue buttercream uses only egg whites, making it very white and easy to color. It's my absolute favorite and soon it will be yours too.

Makes approximately 8 cups (1.2 kg)
(enough to fill, cover and decorate a six-layer 6-inch [15-cm] round cake) ···························

SUGAR SYRUP

1½ cups (300 g) caster sugar or superfine sugar

½ cup (120 g) water

MERINGUE

6 large egg whites

¼ tsp cream of tartar

⅓ cup (66 g) caster sugar or superfine sugar

3 cups (675 g) unsalted butter, softened

1½ tbsp (22 g) vanilla extract

Notes

If your buttercream is too soft, place it in the fridge for 15 minutes and then re-mix.

Meringue-based buttercreams use a large quantity of butter. The higher the quality of the butter, the whiter the buttercream will be and the better it will taste.

It is very important to use caster sugar or superfine sugar in this recipe.

To make the sugar syrup, place the sugar and water in a small saucepan. Stir gently to combine, making sure to not splash the sides of the saucepan. Cook over medium heat using a candy thermometer. The tip of the thermometer should be slightly submerged in the syrup, not touching the bottom of the saucepan.

While the sugar syrup is heating, make the meringue. Beat the egg whites and cream of tartar in a stand mixer on medium speed with the whisk attachment. Once the egg whites are foamy, slowly pour in the sugar and continue beating. Once the sugar syrup reaches 235°F (113°C), immediately remove it from the heat. With the mixer still on medium speed, slowly pour the sugar syrup in a thin stream directly into the meringue between the whisk and side of the bowl. Do not pour it directly onto either. Once incorporated, turn the mixer to high speed and continue mixing until the meringue has cooled, approximately 10 minutes. Meanwhile, the butter should be very soft, but not melted. If it is not soft enough, heat it in the microwave in 10-second increments and mix it together with a spoon until it is the same consistency as peanut butter.

Once the meringue has cooled and the bowl is only slightly warm to touch, turn off the mixer and add all the butter at once. Replace the whisk attachment with the paddle attachment. Mix on low speed until the butter is incorporated, then mix on medium speed for 5 minutes. The meringue will deflate slightly after adding the butter. Add the vanilla and mix on low speed for another 2 minutes. If at any stage the buttercream looks curdled, this is completely normal. Continue mixing and it will come together eventually.

If you would like a colored buttercream, add gel coloring once the butter is incorporated. Start with 5 drops and wait until it's combined, then continue adding 1 to 2 drops at a time until the desired color is achieved To remove any air bubbles from the buttercream, mix it on the lowest setting with the silicone paddle attachment for 5 minutes. Alternatively you can mix it by hand using a silicone spatula.

(continued)

Signature Buttercream (cont.)

FLAVOR VARIATIONS

For a specific flavor, add the below quantities to the buttercream at the same time as the vanilla extract, but reduce the vanilla extract to 2 tsp (10 g). For the lemon and coconut buttercreams, do not add any vanilla extract.

Lemon: 1 tbsp (15 g) lemon extract

Chocolate: 1⅓ cups (226 g) melted and cooled white chocolate or milk chocolate

Caramel: 1 cup (320 g) caramel

Coconut: ¾ cup (180 g) full fat coconut cream and 2 tsp (10 g) coconut extract

Chocolate-hazelnut: 1 cup (300 g) chocolate-hazelnut spread

Peanut butter: 1 cup (250 g) smooth peanut butter

FAVORITE FLAVOR COMBOS

As my cake recipes are already full of flavor, I usually like to frost them with a simple vanilla buttercream. However, these are my other favorite flavor combinations.

Vanilla Cake: white chocolate or caramel Signature Buttercream

Chocolate Cake: white chocolate or vanilla Signature Buttercream

Double Chocolate Cake: milk chocolate or chocolate-hazelnut Signature Buttercream

Caramel Cake: white chocolate or peanut butter Signature Buttercream

Pink Lemonade Cake: lemon Signature Buttercream

Lemon Cake: coconut Signature Buttercream

Coconut Cake: lemon Signature Buttercream

White Chocolate Ganache

Ganache is just so decadent, rich and indulgent. I use the white chocolate version a lot throughout this book, as it can be colored. It can be used at different consistencies to make the most divine filling, frosting or garnish, and it goes with absolutely everything. Basically, it's the ketchup of the baking world.

Makes approximately 1½ cups (315 g) ···

1⅓ cups (226 g) white chocolate

¼ cup plus 2 tbsp (90 g) heavy whipping cream

White gel food coloring (optional)

Gel food coloring in a second color (optional)

Place the white chocolate in a bowl and pour the cream over the top. Heat in the microwave for 30 seconds and then in 10-second increments until the white chocolate has fully melted. Mix well until the ganache is smooth. To color the ganache, first add 2 to 3 drops of white gel coloring and mix until the ganache is white. This will remove the natural yellow tinge of the ganache. Then add 2 to 3 drops of any color gel coloring and mix well to combine.

Decorating Tutorials

Buttercream Basics

If you love smooth sides and sharp edges on your cake, then rejoice! In this tutorial I'll explain just how to achieve them. This method of buttercream application, with its smooth and clean look, will be the base for all my cake decorating tutorials. It's also beautiful on its own if you prefer a simpler look—or want to show off your mad icing skills. Equipment really is everything here. Paired with the right buttercream and technique, you will have the tools to begin your decorating journey where cakes become art. Delicious, mouthwatering art.

Makes one six-layer 6-inch (15-cm) round cake ···

1 batch Vanilla Cake (page 19)

1 batch Signature Buttercream (page 27)

Non-slip silicone mat (usually sold in rolls anywhere that stocks kitchen supplies)

Cake turntable

10-inch (25.5-cm) cake board, minimum 4 mm thick

Angled offset spatulas (small, medium and large)

Large piping bag

Tall cake scraper

Electric/neon pink gel food coloring (optional)

1. Bake the vanilla cakes and chill them overnight, then level them using the method on page 13. The cake layers should be cool before assembly, so remove them from the fridge approximately 15 minutes before beginning to frost the cake.

2. Prepare the buttercream.

3. Place a non-slip mat on your turntable and then a cake board on top. This will ensure the board doesn't move while you are decorating.

4. Use the medium offset spatula to dab some buttercream onto the cake board and spread it slightly, not more than the diameter of the cake. Place the first layer of cake on top (smooth side down) and press down gently.

5. Fill a large piping bag with buttercream and cut off the tip, approximately ½ inch (1 cm). You will need approximately 3½ cups (525 g) of buttercream to fill the layers. Pipe the buttercream onto the cake layer starting from the center. Turning the turntable around with the other hand, continue applying pressure so you make a spiral until you reach the edge of cake, then release. The buttercream layer should be approximately half the height of the cake layer.

6. Use the large offset spatula to smooth the top of the buttercream by holding it still on the buttercream and turning the turntable with your other hand. Place the next layer on top, pressing down very gently. Repeat the process until the final layer. The final layer should have the flat side of the cake facing upwards.

7. Use the medium offset spatula to smooth any buttercream sticking out of the layers and fill in any gaps.

8. Smooth the sides again by holding the tall cake scraper still against the cake on a 45-degree angle and turning the turntable around with the other hand. Do not chill the cake.

9. Squeeze any remaining buttercream from the piping bag back into the mixing bowl with the rest of the buttercream. Add 5 to 6 drops of pink gel coloring, if using, and mix on low speed until combined. Continue adding 2 drops at a time and mixing well at low speed until the desired color is achieved.

(continued)

BUTTERCREAM BASICS (CONT.)

10. Place approximately 1 cup (150 g) of buttercream on top of the cake. To smooth, hold the large offset spatula still on the buttercream and turn the turntable around with your other hand. There will be buttercream hanging off the edge of the cake. Use the medium offset spatula to smooth this excess buttercream onto the sides of the cake.

11. Use the medium offset spatula to cover the entire cake in buttercream.

12. Take the cake scraper and hold it straight to the side of the cake against the buttercream on a 45-degree angle. Holding the scraper in place, begin to slowly turn the turntable with your other hand. Once a full rotation has been done, pull the scraper from the cake and remove the excess buttercream with the medium offset spatula.

13. Fill any gaps with buttercream using the medium offset spatula and begin smoothing again. Once the sides are smooth and even, a lip of buttercream should be sticking up around the top edge of the cake.

14. Place the cake in the freezer for 10 minutes then back onto the turntable. Use the small offset spatula (or a sharp knife) to cut off the lip of buttercream a couple centimeters at a time, by holding the spatula or knife still and turning the turntable with your other hand. If the buttercream begins to soften throughout the process, place the cake in the freezer for 5 minutes before continuing.

15. Once the edges are even and level, smooth the top of the cake by gently scraping the small offset spatula over it.

16. Use a paper towel to clean up excess buttercream on the cake board.

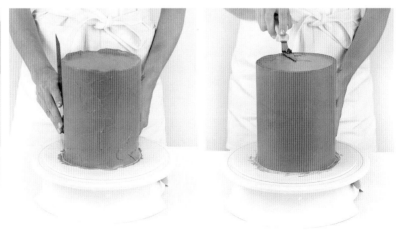

Piping

If you haven't had much experience piping, you'll be an expert by the time you've finished the tutorials in this book. It's amazing how many beautiful designs and patterns can be made to add details to cakes and other desserts. It can be a little overwhelming deciding which tip to use when decorating. Most tips are quite versatile and can be used to make many different designs and patterns. Some tips make the same pattern, but on a different sized scale, such as the star tip. For this reason, it's important to consider what you're using them for. Larger tips work well to cover bigger areas, whereas smaller ones are great for little details and filling in gaps. Listed on page 39 are the tips that I use throughout this book, as well as some of my favorite patterns and designs that each of them makes.

Piping bag

Piping tip

Tall drinking glass

1. Prepare your piping bag by placing the piping tip at the very bottom.

2. Depending on the size of the piping tip, cut off the tip of the bag and pull the piping tip through so that it's secure. For small piping tips, cut off approximately ½ inch (1 cm). For large piping tips, cut off approximately ¾ inch (2 cm).

3. Twist the bottom of the bag just above the tip, so that buttercream doesn't come out while you're filling it.

4. Place the bag into a tall glass and fold the top over the edge of the glass.

5. Scoop the buttercream into the bag using a spoon or silicone spatula. Do not fill the bag all the way to the top, leave at least 4 inches (10 cm).

6. Once the bag is full, hold it in the palm of your hand with the empty top part of the bag in the curve between your thumb and pointer finger. Squeeze your thumb and pointer finger together and push down on the buttercream to move it all to the bottom of the bag and remove any air bubbles, while holding the top of the bag with your other hand.

7. Twist the empty top of the bag and then nestle the bag in your palm, with the twisted top sitting in the curve between your thumb and pointer finger. To begin piping, squeeze the top of the bag that is in your palm. Never squeeze in the middle of the bag or the buttercream will spill out of the top.

(continued)

PIPING (CONT.)

A TRICK FOR MULTICOLOR PIPING

1. Choose three or four colors for your piping. Scoop a small amount of the first color onto the inner side of the piping bag.

2. Continue to scoop a small amount of each color around the inner sides of the bag. You want all colors to fit through the tip at the same time when piping.

3. Once the bottom of the bag has been filled with an even amount of each color, add the remaining buttercream.

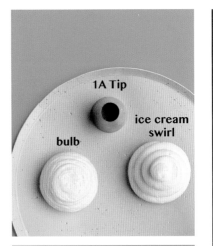

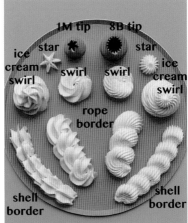

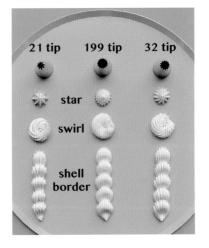

Star: Apply gentle pressure until the buttercream starts coming out of the bag. Once the star is the size you want it, release pressure and pull away.

Swirl: Choose a center point and apply gentle pressure until the buttercream starts coming out of the bag. Keeping the pressure even, slowly make a spiral in a counterclockwise motion. As you reach the outer edge of the cupcake and have made a full circle, release pressure and pull away.

Ice cream swirl: Choose a center point and apply gentle pressure until the buttercream starts coming out of the bag. Keeping the pressure even, slowly make a spiral in a counterclockwise motion. Once you have made a full circle, move the piping bag slightly inward to make the next swirl. Continue this process until you have made a three-layered swirl, the largest at the bottom and the smallest at the top. Once done, release pressure and pull away.

Rope border: Apply gentle pressure until the buttercream starts coming out of the bag. Keeping the pressure even, make a regular swirl. Instead of pulling the bag away once the swirl is done, continue making swirls in the same motion in a downward line, so they are slightly overlapping each other. Once done, release pressure and pull away.

Shell border: Pipe a star using the star method above, but instead of pulling the bag straight up, pull it towards you to make a "tail." Pipe the next star on top of the previous tail and continue the process.

Bulb: Apply gentle pressure until the buttercream starts coming out of the bag. Continue to apply even pressure until the buttercream has spread to the sides, then slowly begin to lift the bag to make a bulb (the tip should be slightly buried in the buttercream). Once you have made a bulb, release pressure and pull away.

White Chocolate Decorations

White chocolate decorations make for the perfect cake toppers. There's nothing like a cake that is entirely edible. I strictly use white compound chocolate to make mine. Firstly, it can be colored unlike milk chocolate. Secondly, compound chocolate does not contain cocoa butter, which means it does not require tempering and hardens quite quickly. This is important when making decorations, as it makes them sturdier, easier to handle and much easier to remove from molds. White chocolate can only be colored with specific chocolate coloring gels or powder, all of which are oil-based. Any coloring that contains water will split and ruin your white chocolate, so take caution not to use them. No one likes sad, split chocolate. I like to use the chocolate coloring ranges from Chefmaster, Color Mill and Rolkem.

1 cup (170 g) compound white chocolate

Chocolate coloring gel or powder (optional)

Silicone mat or parchment paper

Small angled offset spatula

Sprinkles (optional)

Sharp knife

Clothespins

Cutting board

1. Heat the chocolate in the microwave for 30 seconds, then in 15-second increments until it's melted, mixing very well in between. Do not overheat.

2. If you want colored chocolate, add 2 to 3 drops of chocolate coloring gel or a pinch of chocolate coloring powder and mix well to combine.

SHARDS

1. Pour the chocolate over a silicone mat or sheet of parchment paper.

2. Use the offset spatula to spread the chocolate or pick up the silicone mat or parchment and tilt it from side to side until the chocolate is approximately 1/16 inch (2 mm) thick. If you'd like to add sprinkles to the chocolate, do so now.

3. Once the chocolate has almost set, use the knife to score where the chocolate will be cut into triangles. Depending on the temperature of your room, this could happen within a minute or so. The chocolate will no longer be liquid, but will leave an indent if you press on it.

4. Once fully set, use the knife to gently cut through the scored lines and then break off the pieces with your hands. The chocolate will be fully set when it's completely firm to touch.

(continued)

  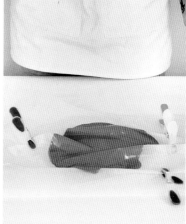

WHITE CHOCOLATE DECORATIONS (CONT.)

SAIL (see photos above)

1. Pour the chocolate over a silicone mat or sheet of parchment paper.

2. Use the offset spatula to spread the chocolate or pick up the silicone mat or parchment paper and tilt it from side to side until the chocolate is approximately $1/16$ inch (2 mm) thick.

3. Scrunch the outer sides of the silicone mat or parchment paper, so the chocolate has a waved effect and use the clothespins to hold them in position.

4. Once fully set, take the clothespins off and peel the chocolate away. Break it into smaller pieces or use the same method to make 2 to 3 individual small sails.

SHAPES (HEARTS, TRIANGLES, CIRCLES, SQUARES, ETC.)

OPTION 1 (see photo to left)

1. You will need a silicone or plastic mold in your chosen shape. Place the mold on a cutting board

2. Pour the melted chocolate into the cavities of the mold and tap the board gently on your countertop.

3. Use the offset spatula to scrape across the top of the mold to remove any excess chocolate.

4. Once fully set, pop the shapes out of the mold by gently pressing on the back.

OPTION 2 (see photos to right)

1. You will need metal cookie cutters in your chosen shape.

2. Prepare the chocolate the same way you would to make shards.

3. Once the chocolate has almost set, gently press the cookie cutter into it enough to make an outline.

4. Once fully set, press the cookie cutter all the way down over the outlines and gently pop the shape from the cutter with your finger.

MARBLING (see photo below)

To make any of the above decorations with a marble effect, simply divide the chocolate into two bowls and color each one individually with 2 to 3 drops of chocolate coloring gel or a pinch of chocolate coloring powder and mix well to combine. Instead of pouring all the chocolate at once, use a spoon to drizzle a little bit of one color and then the other over the top. Continue drizzling with the alternating colors until it's all been used. Pick up the silicone mat or parchment paper and tilt it gently from side to side so the chocolate is spread evenly but without the colors running together too much. Use a toothpick to swirl through the chocolate for a marbled effect.

Sprinkles

Sprinkles are my #1 favorite thing to decorate with. I don't think there's a single decorating tutorial in this book that doesn't include them. For good reason too—sprinkles are life. They just make everything look better, happier and more fun. When I started my baking journey, I thought sprinkles were just sprinkles. No matter what their shape or size was, they all fell under that one category. Right? Wrong! There are so many types and all with distinct features. Then there is the queen of sprinkles—the medley—which is a combination of LOTS of different types. When in doubt, always go for the medley.

Isomalt Crown

A crown is the ultimate cake topper in my opinion, so naturally I had to include one made from isomalt. If you're not familiar with isomalt, it's a shiny, pretty sugar substitute which, once shaped, makes the perfect cake decoration.

Makes one isomalt crown

2 tall drinking glasses

1 cup (200 g) colored or clear isomalt nibs

Silicone mat or parchment paper

Clothespins

Note

If you're not using the isomalt crown immediately, store it in an airtight container. Humidity will make the crown cloudy and sticky.

1. Stack the two drinking glasses on top of each other upside down on a sheet of parchment paper to catch any drips.

2. Heat the isomalt in the microwave for 30 seconds and then in 15-second increments until it's fully melted.

3. Pour the melted isomalt over the silicone mat or parchment paper.

4. Pick up the silicone mat or parchment paper and tilt it from side to side so that the isomalt spreads slightly. Allow it to sit for approximately 45 seconds.

5. Place the silicone mat or parchment paper on top of the stacked glasses and allow the sides to hang over.

6. Reposition the sides until you're happy with the shape it will make and then use the clothespins to secure them.

7. Once fully set, pick up the isomalt crown and gently peel the silicone mat or parchment paper away from it. The time it takes for the isomalt to set will depend on the temperature of your room. It is set once it's no longer sticky to touch.

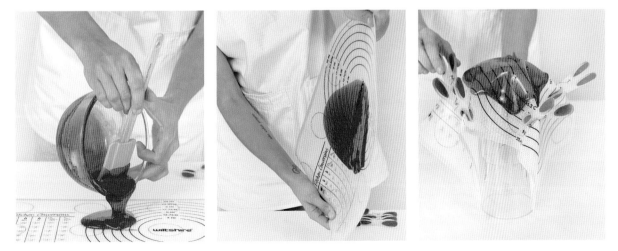

Drip Cake

Nothing shook up the cake world like the drip cake. It was a phenomenon. First done by amazing Aussie baker Katherine Sabbath, inspired by the drips on the cover of *Goosebumps* books, this trend traveled far and wide and has maintained its popularity years later. Basically, it's here to stay. Aside from looking cool, it's also so much fun to make. If you were a fly on a wall in my house while I was making one, you'd see me jumping up and down, clapping and cheering on the drips like they were in a competition. Well, they sort of are. It's like a race down the cake. Trust me, it's entertaining.

Makes one six-layer 6-inch (15-cm) round cake ·······························

1 batch Vanilla Cake (page 19)

1 batch Signature Buttercream (page 27)

Electric/neon orange, pink and purple gel food coloring

½ batch White Chocolate Ganache (page 29)

White gel food coloring

2 piping bags

Cake turntable

Small angled offset spatula

1M piping tip

Blue nonpareils

Rainbow sprinkle medley

1. Bake the vanilla cakes and chill them overnight, then level them using the method on page 13.

2. Prepare the buttercream.

3. Frost the cake using the method on pages 33–34. Before coloring the buttercream for the outer layer of the cake, remove approximately 2½ cups (375 g) and set it aside.

4. Color the buttercream for the outer layer of the cake by adding 5 to 6 drops of orange gel coloring and mixing with the stand mixer on low speed until combined. Continue adding 2 drops at a time and mixing well on low speed until the desired color is reached. Finish icing the cake according to the instructions and chill it in the fridge for 30 minutes.

5. Prepare the ganache. Add 2 to 3 drops of white gel coloring and mix well to combine, then add 2 to 3 drops of pink gel coloring and mix well to combine. Set aside to cool.

6. Once the ganache is cool, but still runny, pour it into a piping bag. Remove the cake from the fridge and place it on the turntable.

7. Cut off the tip of the piping bag, approximately ¼ inch (0.5 cm).

8. For a more even and uniform drip, hold the bag at the top edge of the cake and slowly squeeze it until the ganache starts coming out. The first drip will be a test. If the drip runs all the way to the bottom of the cake, squeeze less next time. If the drip is too short, squeeze more.

9. Hold the bag in one hand and slowly turn the cake turntable around with the other, squeezing to make a drip every ¾ inch (2 cm).

10. Once all the sides have drips, pour the remaining ganache on top of the cake and smooth it out with your offset spatula until it is fully covered.

11. For a more organic and random drip, pour the ganache on top of the cake and use a spoon to gently push it to the edge of the cake until it drips down the side. Repeat all the way around the cake.

12. Chill the cake in the fridge for 15 minutes.

(continued)

DRIP CAKE (CONT.)

13. Take the buttercream that was set aside and color it with 4 to 5 drops of purple gel coloring and mix to combine. Continue adding 1 drop at a time and mixing well until the desired color is reached.

14. Fit the piping bag with the tip and fill it with purple buttercream using the method on page 36.

15. Remove the cake from the fridge and place it on the turntable. Hold the bag directly over the cake and pipe 8 ice cream swirls around the edge of the cake using the method on page 39.

16. Use a spoon to pour blue nonpareils over the buttercream swirls.

17. Use the palm of your hand to gently press rainbow sprinkles into the buttercream all around the bottom of the cake.

18. Use an offset spatula or knife to sweep away any excess sprinkles that have fallen onto the cake board.

Abstract Cake

Abstract cakes are the best, basically because there's no right or wrong way of doing them. You can't mess them up. In fact, they're my go-to method of cake decorating when I mess something else up. Accidently stuck your finger in the cake? Just paint some buttercream over it. Imperfections from the initial smoothing stage? Just paint some buttercream over it. Then call it art. My favorite part of this method is the contrast between the smooth buttercream and textured "paintbrush" streaks. It really stands out and is so much fun, because you don't have to worry about having perfect technique. Anything goes! Yep, you're going to love this one.

Makes one six-layer 6-inch (15-cm) round cake ···

1 batch Chocolate Cake (page 20)

12–13 pink chocolate shards, squares and circles (pages 41 and 42)

1 batch Signature Buttercream (page 27)

Electric/neon green, pink, purple, blue and orange gel food coloring

Cake turntable

Small angled offset spatula

2 piping bags

21 and 32 piping tips

Pink pearl dragees

Purple and pink metallic rods

Rainbow sprinkles

Blue nonpareils

Pink candy balls

1. Bake the chocolate cakes and chill them overnight, then level them using the method on page 13.

2. Make the pink chocolate shapes. Use the method on page 41 to make the shards. Use the first or second method on page 41 or 42 for the squares and circles. Set them aside.

3. Prepare the buttercream.

4. Frost the cake using the method on pages 33–34. Before coloring the buttercream for the outer layer of the cake, remove approximately 1½ cups (225 g) and set it aside.

5. Color the buttercream for the outer layer of the cake by adding 5 to 6 drops of green gel coloring and mixing with the stand mixer on low speed until combined. Continue adding 2 drops at a time and mixing well on low speed until the desired color is reached. Finish icing the cake according to the instructions and chill it in the fridge for 30 minutes.

6. Take the buttercream that was set aside and divide it among four bowls. Color each one individually with 2 to 3 drops of pink, purple, blue and orange gel coloring. Mix each one very well.

7. Remove the cake from the fridge and place it on the turntable. Starting with orange, use the offset spatula to dab streaks onto the front of the cake and spread them in different directions, as if abstract painting (see image on page 50).

8. Wipe the spatula clean and repeat with pink, purple and blue. Clean the spatula between each color application.

9. Fit a piping bag with the 21 tip and fill it with the remaining purple and pink buttercream using the method on page 38.

10. Pipe 4 or 5 swirls over the abstract buttercream using the method on page 39.

11. Fit the other piping bag with the 32 tip and fill it with the remaining blue and orange buttercream using the method on page 38.

(continued)

ABSTRACT CAKE (CONT.)

12. Pipe 10 to 12 stars over the abstract buttercream using the method on page 39.

13. Scatter the different types of sprinkles in patches over the abstract buttercream.

14. Use one of the piping bags to pipe a small star on the back of a pink chocolate shape and stick it to the middle right side of the cake. The piped star will work as "glue" to make the chocolate shape stay in place.

15. Continue adding the pink chocolate shapes up the cake, slightly overlapping each other until you reach the top. Then stick the remaining shapes directly into the top of the cake.

Candy Cake

I have a massive soft spot for candy cakes. One, because the first proper birthday cake I made for my son was a candy cake and I will never forget the look on his face when he saw it. Two, because Blake Lively liked a photo of said cake on Instagram. I took a screenshot of it and pretty much didn't stop showing people or talking about it for weeks (okay, months). Highlight of my career for sure. The candy cake is the epitome of fun and happiness. You absolutely can't look at one and not smile or want to faceplant into it. Also FYI, they are not just for children. I've had just as many adults order candy cakes for themselves. Love for candy doesn't stop when you become an adult. In fact, it probably strengthens, because you have your own money to buy as much as you want and no one is going to tell you off for eating too much of it—fact!

Makes one six-layer 6-inch (15-cm) round cake ···

1 batch Vanilla Cake (page 19)

White chocolate bar (made with mold using method on page 42)

2 paintbrushes

Edible glue (from any cake decorating supply store)

Silver edible glitter

¼ cup (42 g) white chocolate

Pink chocolate coloring gel or powder

Ice cream cone (pointed bottom)

1 batch Signature Buttercream (page 27)

Electric/neon green and blue gel food coloring

Piping bag

1M piping tip

Cake turntable

Candy (chocolate bars, jellies, novelty candy, lollipops, etc.)

Rainbow sprinkles

1. Bake the vanilla cakes and chill them overnight, then level them using the method on page 13.

2. Make the white chocolate bar using the method on page 42. Once set, use a paintbrush to cover the chocolate bar with a thin layer of edible glue. Then use the other paintbrush to paint on the glitter. Chocolate bar molds can be found online. If you're unable to acquire one, you can use a store-bought white chocolate bar. Set aside the bar to dry.

3. Place the white chocolate in a very small bowl or drinking glass and heat in the microwave for 30 seconds, then in 15-second increments until it's fully melted. Add 2 to 3 drops of pink chocolate coloring gel or a pinch of pink chocolate coloring powder and mix well to combine. Dip the rim of the ice cream cone into the chocolate and then hold it upright so the chocolate drips slightly. Place the cone into a drinking glass or the top of an empty water bottle so that it remains upright and set it aside.

4. Prepare the buttercream.

5. Remove approximately ⅔ cup (100 g) of buttercream and add 2 to 3 drops of green gel coloring. Mix to combine.

6. Fit the piping bag with the tip and fill it with green buttercream using the method on page 36.

7. Hold your ice cream cone in one hand and the piping bag over it with the other. Apply gentle pressure to the bag until buttercream starts coming out and allow the cone to fill. Once the buttercream has reached the rim of the cone, begin to make an ice cream swirl using the method on page 39. Place the cone back into the drinking glass or water bottle and chill it in the fridge.

(continued)

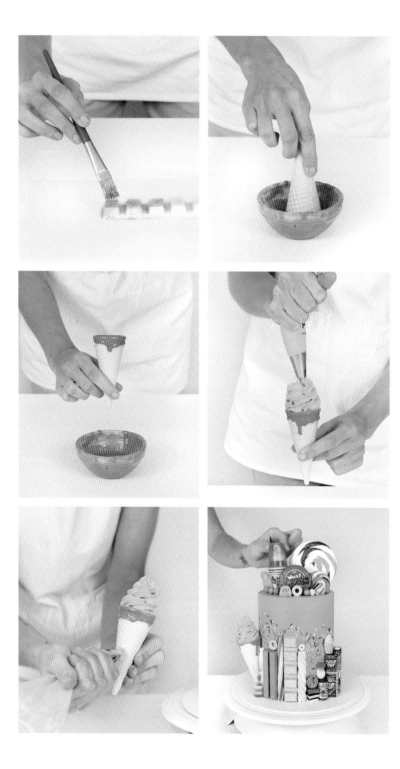

CANDY CAKE (CONT.)

8. Ice the cake using the method on pages 33–34. Color the buttercream for the outer layer by adding 5 to 6 drops of blue gel coloring and mixing with the stand mixer on low speed until combined. Continue adding 2 drops at a time and mixing well on low speed until the desired color is reached. Once the cake is fully iced, chill it in the fridge for 15 minutes.

9. Remove the cake from the fridge and place it on the turntable. The buttercream should be soft enough that you can stick pieces of candy to it, but firm enough for the candy to not smudge it.

10. Starting at the front and middle of the cake, add the glitter chocolate bar. If it doesn't stick to the cake securely, dab some buttercream to the back of it, which will work as "glue."

11. Continue adding pieces of candy around the bottom of the cake at different heights, some stacked on top of each other.

12. Stick the cone to the left side of the cake, using extra buttercream as "glue" if required.

13. Once the bottom of the cake has been covered all the way around, scatter sprinkles onto the buttercream that is still showing.

14. On the top of the cake, add the remaining candy, starting with the largest at the back and the smallest at the front so that they are all in view.

15. Chill the cake in the fridge immediately so that all the candy remains stuck securely.

Splatter Cake

This design is perfect for when you don't want too many decorations on your cake, but you don't want it too simple either. I personally love it because it adds just a little more buttercream to the outer layer. Any excuse for extra buttercream, I say. It's also versatile in the way the colors are used. For a more elegant and simple effect, I use various shades of the same color. When I want the cake to really stand out and look fun, I use three or four different colors.

Makes one six-layer 6-inch (15-cm) round cake ··

1 batch Lemon Cake (page 21)

½ cup (85 g) compound white chocolate

Yellow chocolate coloring gel or powder

Piping bag

Parchment paper

Pink isomalt crown (page 45)

1 batch coconut Signature Buttercream (page 27)

Electric/neon pink and purple gel food coloring

Cake turntable

Small angled offset spatula

Tall cake scraper

Paintbrush

Edible orange paint

1. Bake the lemon cakes and chill them overnight, then level them using the method on page 13.

2. Melt the chocolate in the microwave for 30 seconds, then in 15-second increments until it's fully melted. Add 2 to 3 drops of yellow chocolate coloring gel or a pinch of yellow chocolate coloring powder and mix well to combine.

3. Pour the chocolate into the piping bag and cut off the tip, approximately ⅛ inch (3 mm). On a sheet of parchment paper, drizzle the chocolate to make one continuous "tangled squiggle" and place it aside to set.

4. Make the isomalt crown using the method on page 45 and set it aside.

5. Prepare the coconut buttercream.

6. Frost the cake using the method on pages 33–34 without coloring the buttercream for the outer layer and place it in the freezer for 5 minutes.

7. Divide the remaining buttercream into two bowls and color each one individually with 3 to 4 drops of pink and purple gel coloring. Mix each one well to combine. At this stage, the softer the buttercream, the easier it will be to smear.

8. Remove the cake from the freezer and place it on the turntable. Starting with the pink buttercream, use the offset spatula to thinly smear it in patches all over the cake.

9. Hold the cake scraper still with one hand against the side of the cake until it only just makes contact with the buttercream smears, and with the other hand, slowly turn the cake turntable. The cake scraper should not make contact with the smooth layer of white buttercream.

10. Place the cake in the freezer for 5 minutes, then repeat the process with the purple buttercream. Fill in any white gaps as much as possible, but try not to have the colors overlap and blend into each other too much.

(continued)

11. Once you have finished smearing on the buttercream, use the cake scraper to smooth the cake over one final time very lightly so the colors don't blend. If throughout the process the buttercream is softening too much, place the cake in the freezer for 5 minutes before continuing. Once the cake is smooth, chill it in the fridge for 15 minutes.

12. Remove the cake from the fridge and place it on the turntable. Dip the paintbrush into the edible orange paint and splatter it over the cake by tapping the paintbrush against your finger. Chill the cake in the fridge for 10 minutes to allow the paint to dry.

13. Remove the cake from the fridge and place it on the turntable. Gently peel the chocolate squiggle from the parchment paper. Place it at the front of the cake, pressing gently so that it sticks to the buttercream.

14. Dab a small amount of buttercream on top of the cake and then gently stick the isomalt crown to it.

Note

The moisture from the fridge will make the isomalt crown cloudy, so it's best to place it on top of the cake just before serving or displaying.

Stencil Cake

I can't begin to tell you how fun this cake is to make. I tend to steer clear of overly themed cakes, but these are just perfect to tie in with a theme, without it being overkill. It's all about balance, people. Also, it's almost entirely covered in sprinkles—need I say more? All you need is a stencil to match your theme. The stenciled shapes look beautiful on their own, but the sprinkles really make the cake pop. In saying that, I take no responsibility for the sprinkles that you will still be finding in various parts of your kitchen months after making this.

Makes one six-layer 6-inch (15-cm) round cake ···

1 batch Pink Lemonade Cake (page 23)

1 batch lemon Signature Buttercream (page 27)

Electric/neon pink and purple gel food coloring

Heart-shaped cookie cutter, optional

Parchment paper

Scissors

Cake turntable

Large baking tray with high sides

2 cups (400 g) sprinkles (different colored medleys, sprinkles, non-pareils, etc.)

4 piping bags

32, 199, 21 and 1M piping tips

Silver edible glitter

1. Bake the pink lemonade cakes and chill them overnight, then level them using the method on page 13.

2. Prepare the lemon buttercream.

3. Frost the cake using the method on pages 33–34. Color the buttercream for the outer layer of the cake by adding 5 to 6 drops of pink gel coloring and mixing with the stand mixer on low speed until combined. Continue adding 2 drops at a time and mixing well on low speed until the desired color is reached. Once the cake is fully iced, chill it in the fridge for 15 minutes.

4. Trace a heart onto the sheet of parchment paper using a cookie cutter or a printout that's approximately 4 x 4 inches (10 x 10 cm). Cut out the heart.

5. Remove the cake from the fridge and place it on the turntable. Gently place the heart stencil at the front and center of the cake. Use your fingers to smooth it over so that it is flat against the buttercream.

6. Place the cake turntable with the cake on top into the baking tray. The baking tray will catch the excess sprinkles.

7. Pour some sprinkles into the palm of your hand and gently push them onto the cake. Alternate the types and colors of sprinkles after every application so that there are different patches of sprinkles around the cake. Continue adding the sprinkles until all the sides are covered, but not the top of the cake. If the buttercream starts softening too much during the decorating process, place it in the fridge for 10 minutes before continuing.

8. Once all the sides are covered, carefully remove the heart stencil and chill the cake in the fridge while you prepare the buttercream. The stencil is removed more easily with tweezers.

9. Divide the remaining buttercream among three bowls. Add one drop of pink coloring to one, two drops to the next and leave the last one as is. Mix each one well until combined to have three shades of pink.

(continued)

STENCIL CAKE (CONT.)

10. Fit three piping bags with tips 32, 199 and 21 and fill each with a different shade of pink, using the method on page 36.

11. Starting with the 32 tip, pipe 8 to 9 swirls into the heart shape using the method on page 39. Fill in any gaps using the 199 and 21 tips to pipe small stars using the method on page 39.

12. Squeeze the remaining pink buttercreams evenly between two bowls. Add 2 to 3 drops of purple gel coloring to one bowl and mix well to combine so that you make a fuchsia color. Fit the last piping bag with the 1M tip and fill it with the remaining pink and fuchsia buttercream using the method on page 38.

13. Hold the piping bag above the cake at a 45-degree angle with one hand and pipe a continuous rope around the edge using the method on page 39 while turning the cake table with the other hand.

14. Use a spoon to sprinkle glitter over the buttercream rope border.

Unicorn Cake

I strongly dislike making unicorn cakes and avoid making them at all costs. Not that they aren't beautiful, I just felt I was limited in how creative I could get with them. Ironically, that is how I came up with this utterly fabulous idea. A very good friend wanted a unicorn cake for her daughter's birthday, and I couldn't say no. I was against the idea of the fondant horn though and desperately needed an alternative. I went through my pantry searching for a solution and stumbled across some ice cream cones and sprinkles—and with those, a star was born.

Makes one six-layer 6-inch (15-cm) round cake ··

1 batch Coconut Cake (page 24)

¼ cup (60 g) white fondant

Rolling pin

Parchment paper

¾ cup (127 g) white chocolate

Pink chocolate coloring gel or powder

1 ice cream cone (pointed bottom)

Rainbow sprinkle medley

1 batch white chocolate Signature Buttercream (page 27)

Electric/neon pink, purple, yellow, blue and green gel food coloring

Cake turntable

Glitter dusting pump (optional)

Pink edible glitter or luster dust (optional)

Ruler

Sharp knife

Pink metallic rods

4 piping bags

1M, 199, 21 and 32 piping tips

Pink edible pen

1. Bake the coconut cakes and chill them overnight, then level them using the method on page 13.

2. Prepare the horn and ears. Roll out the fondant onto parchment paper until it's approximately ⅛ inch (3 mm) thick and set it aside to dry out slightly.

3. Melt the chocolate in a large shallow bowl for 30 seconds, then in 15-second increments until it's melted. Add one drop of pink chocolate coloring gel or a pinch of pink chocolate coloring powder and mix well to combine. Lay the cone on its side in the chocolate and roll it with your fingers until it's fully coated. Place the cone onto a sheet of parchment paper (pointed end up) and cover it with sprinkles (see images on page 62). Allowing the chocolate to set slightly first will prevent the sprinkles from dripping down the cone. The chocolate should be soft, but not runny. Place it aside to set.

4. With the remaining chocolate, make a circle for the eyes approximately 1 inch (3 cm) in diameter using the first or second method on page 42 or 43 and set it aside.

5. Prepare the white chocolate buttercream.

6. Frost the cake using the method on pages 33–34. Before coloring the buttercream for the outer layer of the cake, remove approximately 3 cups (450 g) and set it aside.

7. Color the buttercream for the outer layer of the cake by adding 5 to 6 drops of pink gel coloring and mixing with the stand mixer on low speed until combined. Continue adding 2 drops at a time and mixing well on low speed until the desired color is reached. Finish icing the cake according to the instructions and chill it in the fridge for 10 minutes.

8. Remove the cake from the fridge and place it on the turntable. Fill the dusting pump with glitter or luster dust and spray the entire cake, then place it back in the fridge to chill. This step can be skipped if you don't have a pump.

9. Divide the buttercream that was set aside into four bowls and color each one individually with 2 to 3 drops of purple, yellow, blue and green gel coloring. Mix each one well to combine.

10. Remove the cake from the fridge and place it on the turntable. Hold a ruler in front of the cake as a level guide, and gently make two indents where the eyes will be.

(continued)

UNICORN CAKE (CONT.)

11. Take the pink chocolate circle and use the knife to score a line directly through the middle. Do not cut the whole way through. Pick up the circle and use your hands to break it in half along the line. Gently press each half onto the indents for the eyes with the curved parts facing up, then place three metallic rods on the outer edge of each eye for the eyelashes. Chill the cake in the fridge for 5 minutes to allow the eyes to set.

12. Fit the piping bags with the tips and fill each one with two or three different colored buttercreams, including any leftover pink buttercream, using the method on page 38.

13. Remove the cake from the fridge and place it on the turntable. Use the 199 tip to pipe a small star that's centered and just above the eyes. Alternate the piping tips to pipe colored swirls or stars up the forehead to make an upside-down triangle using the methods on page 39.

14. Once you reach the top edge of the cake, continue piping the top middle section, leaving the side edges bare.

15. Once the top of the cake has been piped, turn the cake table so the back of the cake is facing you and continue piping the "mane" down the back of the cake. As you reach the bottom of the cake, begin to pipe to one side, so that the bottom of the "mane" will be visible from the front.

16. Use a spoon to pour sprinkles over the top and back of the "mane" and your fingers to stick some to the front. Chill the cake in the fridge while you make the ears.

17. Use the knife to cut out two ears from the fondant, then color the insides pink with the edible pen.

18. Remove the cake from the fridge and place it on the turntable. Place the horn on top by pressing it gently into the buttercream "mane" and the ears on each side of it.

Color Block Cake

This is probably my favorite style of cake. It's such a versatile design, because depending on what you add to it and the colors you use, it can be fun, elegant, pretty, simple, cute, crazy . . . okay, you get my point. Also, I LOVE piping and there's plenty of that. The piped block looks absolutely beautiful on its own and is a great way to showcase your piping skills, but if you want to be a little extra, you can also add some sprinkles or candy to it. I pretty much always do this, because we have established I don't know when to stop. I'm not one to peer pressure, so it's your call, but . . . go big or go home, I reckon.

Makes one six-layer 6-inch (15-cm) round cake ···

1 batch Caramel Cake (page 25)

Pink chocolate sails (page 42)

Paintbrush

Pink luster dust

1 batch white chocolate Signature Buttercream (page 27)

Turquoise gel food coloring

Electric/neon pink gel food coloring

4 piping bags

1M, 8B, 32 and 199 piping tips

Cake turntable

Pink sprinkles

Candy balls or gumballs (optional)

1. Bake the caramel cakes and chill them overnight, then level them using the method on page 13.

2. Make the chocolate sails using the method on page 42. Once set, use the paintbrush to powder luster dust over them.

3. Prepare the white chocolate buttercream.

4. Frost the cake using the method on pages 33–34. Before coloring the buttercream for the outer layer of the cake, remove approximately 2½ cups (375 g) and set it aside.

5. Color the buttercream for the outer layer of the cake by adding 5 to 6 drops of turquoise gel coloring and mixing with the stand mixer on low speed until combined. Continue adding 2 drops at a time and mixing well on low speed until the desired color is reached. Finish icing the cake according to the instructions and then chill it in the fridge.

6. Divide the buttercream that was set aside among four bowls. Add one drop of pink coloring to the first, two drops to the second, three drops to the third and four drops to the last. Mix each one well to have four shades of pink.

7. Fit the piping bags with tips 1M, 8B, 32 and 199 and fill each with a different shade of pink, using the method on page 36.

8. Remove the cake from the fridge and place it on the turntable. Starting with the 1M tip, pipe 5 or 6 swirls onto the front of the cake, 7 or 8 stars with the 8B tip, and 6 or 7 swirls with the 32 tip, using the methods on page 39. This should form a "block" of buttercream from the bottom of the cake to the top edge. Use the 199 tip to pipe small stars to fill in any gaps. The 32 tip can also be used to pipe small stars.

9. Scatter sprinkles sparingly over the pink buttercream, not covering the details of the piping too much.

10. Gently stick the chocolate sails into the top of the cake, deep enough that they are stable. For added stability, stick some candy balls or gumballs behind them.

Keep Calm and Eat Cupcakes

Cupcakes hold a special place in my heart. I really took my baking skills and business to the next level when I started making them. They're something I'd often made as a kid—usually from a box mix and always tasting better than they looked—but a few years ago they opened a whole new world to me. The options were endless in terms of flavors, buttercreams, textures and decorations. It allowed me to experiment and let my creativity flow. I loved making something that looked as good as it tasted, that made people smile to see them as much as it did to eat them.

Once I started offering cupcakes on my menu, I quickly found that people loved their versatility. What may have once been thought of as just a children's treat had become the focal point of dessert tables—even at adult parties. Thanks to the various piping methods and decorations, cupcakes were being made to match color schemes or party themes, and their designs were now being appreciated as equally as their taste. Cupcake bakers had become artists.

Someone once told me that eating one of my cupcakes could be compared to eating a rainbow (I think they'd had one too many and were on a sugar high). I found this analogy interesting and kept it in the back of my mind every time I made cupcakes from that point on. I wanted people, in addition to loving the taste, to also acknowledge the design and details that lovingly went into them and feel the same way that woman did.

This next chapter will provide hours of fun, with cupcake creations that even the most inexperienced baker will master. Along with my favorite cupcake recipes, there are step-by-step tutorials on how to decorate them. I must tell you though, I can take no responsibility if anyone becomes addicted to piping cupcakes. Once mastered, it is a very enjoyable and almost therapeutic process. You have been warned. . . .

Vanilla Cupcakes

The vanilla cupcake is a staple recipe that everyone should have. It's a great foundation to experiment with other flavor variations, yet so many people struggle to find the perfect one. The biggest cupcake sin is dryness. Even a mountain of buttercream can't save a dry cupcake. Another is cupcakes that are too airy. I like to call really airy cupcakes "non-cupcakes." They're practically imaginary, with no flavor. At that point I'd rather walk around with my mouth open and eat air. I'd save on the calories too. No, I need something I can really sink my teeth into! I therefore present to you my vanilla cupcake. A strong butter and vanilla flavor, with richness from the added egg yolk and moistness from the yogurt. You definitely need this one in your life.

Makes approximately 12 regular cupcakes

1¼ cups (156 g) all-purpose flour

1½ tsp (6 g) baking powder

½ tsp salt

½ cup (113 g) unsalted butter, melted and cooled

1 cup (200 g) caster sugar or superfine sugar

1 large egg, plus 1 yolk

⅔ cup (160 g) full fat milk

3 tbsp (45 g) full fat Greek yogurt

1 tbsp (15 g) vegetable oil

2 tsp (10 g) vanilla extract

Preheat the oven to 300°F (150°C). Place cupcake liners into a cupcake pan.

In a large bowl, whisk together the flour, baking powder and salt. In a medium bowl, whisk together the butter and sugar until combined. Add the egg, egg yolk, milk, yogurt, oil and extract. Whisk again to combine. Pour the wet ingredients into the dry ingredients and whisk until just combined. Do not overmix.

Use an ice cream scoop to fill the liners with batter, about two-thirds full, and place the tray in the oven on the middle rack. Bake for 25 to 30 minutes, rotating the tray halfway through.

Regular cupcake pans can vary slightly in size, so the bake time will depend on this. Check for doneness at 25 minutes by inserting a toothpick into a cupcake. If it comes out clean, the cupcakes are ready. Once baked, remove the cupcakes immediately from the pan and onto a cooling rack. Allow them to cool completely before decorating.

Chocolate Cupcakes

If you don't like chocolate cupcakes, then I feel your pain. I understand this, because that used to be me. I've always been Team Vanilla, which is interesting because I love chocolate more than I even love cake! Chocolate cupcakes had just never satisfied me and always left something to be desired. Chocolate is the ultimate happy food, as science has proven, and I absolutely had to experience the happiness of eating a chocolate cupcake at least once in my life. I played around with popular recipes, but found they were either too airy or too heavy. I needed something in between that had the perfect texture and a good chocolate flavor without being overpowering. Basically, I needed a chocolate version of my vanilla cupcake—how hard could it be? LIGHTBULB MOMENT! The answer had been in front of me the whole time. I made one change to my vanilla recipe and ta-da! A moist and smooth texture with a perfectly rich and decadent chocolate flavor. I'm finally a chocolate-cupcake lover.

Makes approximately 12 regular cupcakes

1 cup (125 g) all-purpose flour

⅓ cup (33 g) unsweetened cocoa powder

1½ tsp (6 g) baking powder

½ tsp salt

½ cup (113 g) unsalted butter, melted and cooled

1 cup (200 g) caster sugar or superfine sugar

1 large egg, plus 1 yolk

⅔ cup (160 g) full fat milk

3 tbsp (45 g) full fat Greek yogurt

1 tbsp (15 g) vegetable oil

1 tsp vanilla extract

1 tbsp (15 g) hot water

Preheat the oven to 300°F (150°C). Place cupcake liners into a cupcake pan.

In a large bowl, sift together the flour, cocoa, baking powder and salt. In a medium bowl, whisk together the butter and sugar until combined. Add the egg, egg yolk, milk, yogurt, oil and vanilla extract. Whisk again to combine. Pour the wet ingredients into the dry ingredients. As you're whisking the wet and dry ingredients together, add the hot water. Whisk until just combined. Do not overmix.

Use an ice cream scoop to fill the liners with batter, about two-thirds full, and place the tray in the oven on the middle rack. Bake for 25 to 30 minutes, rotating the tray halfway through.

Regular cupcake pans can vary slightly in size, so the bake time will depend on this. Check for doneness at 25 minutes by inserting a toothpick into a cupcake. If it comes out clean, the cupcakes are ready. Once baked, remove the cupcakes immediately from the pan and onto a cooling rack. Allow them to cool completely before decorating.

Lemon Cupcakes

They say that when life gives you lemons, you should make lemonade. That's great, but I'd rather make cupcakes. Lemon-flavored cupcakes were not enticing to me until a few years ago when I started experimenting with them myself. It's one of those flavors where you need to have just the right amount. Not enough, and it fails to even be lemon-flavored. Too much and it makes you have facial spasms. Lemons are naturally sour after all. This is my Goldilocks lemon cupcake; not too plain, not too sour, perfectly sweet, a little bit tangy and overall just right.

Makes approximately 12 regular cupcakes ···

1¼ cups (156 g) all-purpose flour

1½ tsp (6 g) baking powder

½ tsp salt

½ cup (113 g) unsalted butter, melted and cooled

1 cup (200 g) caster sugar or superfine sugar

½ tbsp (3 g) lemon zest

1 large egg, plus 1 yolk

⅔ cup (160 g) full fat milk

3 tbsp (45 g) full fat Greek yogurt

1 tbsp (15 g) vegetable oil

2 tsp (10 g) lemon extract

Preheat the oven to 300°F (150°C). Place cupcake liners into a cupcake pan.

In a large bowl, whisk together the flour, baking powder and salt. In a medium bowl, whisk together the butter, sugar and zest until combined. Add the egg, egg yolk, milk, yogurt, oil and lemon extract. Whisk again to combine. Pour the wet ingredients into the dry ingredients and whisk until just combined. Do not overmix.

Use an ice cream scoop to fill the liners with batter, about two-thirds full, and place the tray in the oven on the middle rack. Bake for 25 to 30 minutes, rotating the tray halfway through.

Regular cupcake pans can vary slightly in size, so the bake time will depend on this. Check for doneness at 25 minutes by inserting a toothpick into a cupcake. If it comes out clean, the cupcakes are ready. Once baked, remove the cupcakes immediately from the pan and onto a cooling rack. Allow them to cool completely before decorating.

Pink Lemonade Cupcakes

You know when you hear parents joke that one of their kids was an accident, but they're so happy about it and love that child to death? Well it's the same with these cupcakes. I wanted to make a recipe for a cake but tested it on a smaller scale first. They were AMAZING! My pink lemonade cupcake was officially born. Years later, they're my best-selling cupcake flavor. Sweet, lemony and perfectly pink.

Makes approximately 12 regular cupcakes ···

1¼ cups (156 g) all-purpose flour

1½ tsp (6 g) baking powder

½ tsp salt

½ cup (113 g) unsalted butter, melted and cooled

1 cup (200 g) caster sugar or superfine sugar

1 large egg, plus 1 yolk

⅔ cup (160 g) full fat milk

3 tbsp (45 g) full fat Greek yogurt

1 tbsp (15 g) vegetable oil

½ tbsp (7.5 g) lemon extract

½ tsp cotton candy flavoring

Electric/neon pink gel food coloring

Preheat the oven to 300ºF (150ºC). Place cupcake liners into a cupcake pan.

In a large bowl, whisk together the flour, baking powder and salt. In a medium bowl, whisk together the butter and sugar until combined. Add the egg, egg yolk, milk, yogurt, oil, lemon extract, cotton candy flavoring and 2 to 3 drops of pink gel coloring. Whisk again to combine. Pour the wet ingredients into the dry ingredients and whisk until just combined. Do not overmix.

Use an ice cream scoop to fill the liners with batter, about three-quarters full, and place the tray in the oven on the middle rack. Bake for 25 to 30 minutes, rotating the tray halfway through.

Regular cupcake pans can vary slightly in size, so the bake time will depend on this. Check for doneness at 25 minutes by inserting a toothpick into a cupcake. If it comes out clean, the cupcakes are ready. Once baked, remove the cupcakes immediately from the pan and onto a cooling rack. Allow them to cool completely before decorating.

Coconut Cupcakes

If you asked me what my favorite childhood memories were, coconuts would be in the top five. Coming home after school to see that Mum had bought a coconut was the child equivalent to winning the lotto. Even now, remembering the way she would make a hole with a screwdriver, pour out the water and then crack it open, gives me warm fuzzies. Once I started baking, I knew I had to have a coconut cupcake. They began as vanilla cupcakes, switching the vanilla extract for coconut. Then I decided I needed to take the situation more seriously. In came the coconut milk and shredded coconut for that triple flavor kick. It's a coconut party for your taste buds.

Makes approximately 12 regular cupcakes ·

1¼ cups (156 g) all-purpose flour

1½ tsp (6 g) baking powder

½ tsp salt

½ cup (113 g) unsalted butter, melted and cooled

1 cup (200 g) caster sugar or superfine sugar

½ cup (40 g) shredded coconut

1 large egg, plus 1 yolk

⅔ cup (160 g) full fat canned coconut milk, room temperature

3 tbsp (45 g) full fat Greek yogurt

1 tbsp (15 g) vegetable oil

1 tsp coconut extract

Preheat the oven to 300ºF (150ºC). Place cupcake liners into a cupcake pan.

In a large bowl, whisk together the flour, baking powder and salt. In a medium bowl, whisk together the butter, sugar and shredded coconut until combined. Add the egg, egg yolk, milk, yogurt, oil and coconut extract. Whisk again to combine. Pour the wet ingredients into the dry ingredients and whisk until just combined. Do not overmix.

Use an ice cream scoop to fill the liners with batter, about two-thirds full, and place the tray in the oven on the middle rack. Bake for 25 to 30 minutes, rotating the tray halfway through.

Regular cupcake pans can vary slightly in size, so the bake time will depend on this. Check for doneness at 25 minutes by inserting a toothpick into a cupcake. If it comes out clean, the cupcakes are ready. Once baked, remove the cupcakes immediately from the pan and onto a cooling rack. Allow them to cool completely before decorating.

Peanut Butter Cupcakes

Peanut butter is my ultimate comfort food. I will eat that stuff right out of the jar like ice cream. (Don't judge, I know you all have too.) It's widely regarded as healthy, which is what I love about it the most, although I think this refers to small quantities and not an entire jar in one sitting. Peanut butter makes anything you add it to SO MUCH BETTER! I mean, it makes celery taste amazing for crying out loud. That's one magic spread right there. So obviously, when you add it to an already delicious cupcake, you have a match made in heaven. Disclaimer: To avoid overconsumption of peanut butter cupcakes, give away to friends and family ASAP.

Makes approximately 12 regular cupcakes

1¼ cups (156 g) all-purpose flour

1½ tsp (6 g) baking powder

½ tsp salt

⅓ cup (75 g) unsalted butter, melted and cooled

1 cup (200 g) light brown sugar, packed

½ cup (125 g) smooth peanut butter

1 large egg, plus 1 yolk

⅔ cup (160 g) full fat milk

3 tbsp (45 g) full fat Greek yogurt

1 tbsp (15 g) vegetable oil

1 tsp vanilla extract

Preheat the oven to 300ºF (150ºC). Place cupcake liners into a cupcake pan.

In a large bowl, whisk together the flour, baking powder and salt. In a medium bowl, whisk together the butter, sugar and peanut butter until combined. Add the egg, egg yolk, milk, yogurt, oil and vanilla extract. Whisk again to combine. Pour the wet ingredients into the dry ingredients and whisk until just combined. Do not overmix.

Use an ice cream scoop to fill the liners with batter, about two-thirds full, and place the tray in the oven on the middle rack. Bake for 25 to 30 minutes, rotating the tray halfway through.

Regular cupcake pans can vary slightly in size, so the bake time will depend on this. Check for doneness at 25 minutes by inserting a toothpick into a cupcake. If it comes out clean, the cupcakes are ready. Once baked, remove the cupcakes immediately from the pan and onto a cooling rack. Allow them to cool completely before decorating.

Chocolate-Hazelnut Cupcakes

If you search "Nutella cupcake recipes" on the Internet, the majority of them are just chocolate cupcakes with Nutella centers. I'm sorry, but this is not good enough. Chocolate-hazelnut spread is one of the most popular foods in the world. It's in pizza, crepes, ice cream. We even have World Nutella Day for goodness' sake. It definitely deserves its own cupcake! It probably deserves its own country, or at least a theme park. That's my idea of happiness right there! Until then, the cupcakes will suffice.

Makes approximately 12 regular cupcakes

1 cup (125 g) all-purpose flour

⅓ cup (33 g) unsweetened cocoa powder

1½ tsp (6 g) baking powder

½ tsp salt

½ cup (113 g) unsalted butter, melted and cooled

1 cup (200 g) caster sugar or superfine sugar

⅓ cup (100 g) chocolate-hazelnut spread, such as Nutella

1 large egg, plus 1 yolk

⅔ cup (160 g) full fat milk

3 tbsp (45 g) full fat Greek yogurt

1 tbsp (15 g) vegetable oil

1 tsp vanilla extract

1 tbsp (15 g) hot water

Preheat the oven to 300°F (150°C). Place cupcake liners into a cupcake pan.

In a large bowl, whisk together the flour, cocoa, baking powder and salt. In a medium bowl, whisk together the butter, sugar and chocolate-hazelnut spread until combined. Add the egg, egg yolk, milk, yogurt, oil and extract. Whisk again to combine. Pour the wet ingredients into the dry ingredients. As you're whisking the wet and dry ingredients together, add the hot water. Whisk until just combined. Do not overmix.

Use an ice cream scoop to fill the liners with batter, about two-thirds full, and place the tray in the oven on the middle rack. Bake for 25 to 30 minutes, rotating the tray halfway through.

Regular cupcake pans can vary slightly in size, so the bake time will depend on this. Check for doneness at 25 minutes by inserting a toothpick into a cupcake. If it comes out clean, the cupcakes are ready. Once baked, remove the cupcakes immediately from the pan and onto a cooling rack. Allow them to cool completely before decorating.

Fancy American Buttercream

This buttercream really excites me. Looking at it, you'd think it were a meringue-based buttercream. It is in fact a simple American buttercream, just a bit fancier. It's so smooth and silky and has little grit and air bubbles unlike a lot of American buttercreams. There's something special about traditional American buttercream. Every time I make it, it takes me back to my childhood. Remember being at parties when the cake would come out and all the adults would surround it like bodyguards protecting a celebrity, holding all the kids back from sticking their fingers in it? Fun times. My mum actually still does the finger sticking. Anyway, back then meringue-based buttercreams weren't all the rage like they are now—American buttercream was #1. I mean, sugar and butter, is there honestly anything better? It's just classic. Unfortunately, a lot of people like to diss it (buttercream snobs). It's often regarded as too sweet or too grainy or too stiff. Well this buttercream is none of those. It's smooth, but holds its shape well, and is not sickly sweet. It's an absolute dream to pipe with and eat, all thanks to a few secret ingredients.

Makes enough buttercream for 12 regular cupcakes

½ cup (113 g) salted butter, softened

1 cup (227 g) unsalted butter, softened

½ cup (150 g) sweetened condensed milk, chilled (see notes)

1 tbsp (15 g) vanilla extract

1 tbsp (10 g) meringue powder (see notes)

2 cups (250 g) powdered sugar, sifted, divided

Cut the butter into cubes and place them into the bowl of a stand mixer. Beat the butter with the paddle attachment on medium speed for 5 minutes. You can also use a hand mixer. Occasionally scrape down the bowl. With the mixer still running, slowly pour in the condensed milk and vanilla extract and continue mixing on medium speed for 2 minutes.

Add the meringue powder and ½ cup (62 g) of the powdered sugar. Mix on low speed until fully incorporated, approximately 1 minute. Repeat this step until all the powdered sugar is combined and then mix on low-medium speed for 5 minutes.

If you would like a colored buttercream, add gel coloring once the sugar is incorporated. Start with 2 drops and wait until it's combined, then continue adding 1 drop at a time until the desired color is achieved. To remove any air bubbles from the buttercream, mix it on the lowest setting with the silicone paddle attachment for 2 to 3 minutes. Alternatively you can mix it by hand using a silicone spatula.

Notes

The condensed milk must be very cold. This enables it to whip better. Leftover milk can be stored in the fridge in an airtight container for up to two weeks.

Do not omit the meringue powder. This is what gives the buttercream the stability it would normally get from a larger amount of powdered sugar.

FLAVOR VARIATIONS

For a specific flavor, reduce the vanilla extract to 1 tsp and add the following amounts to finished buttercream. Mix on low speed for 2 minutes to combine.

Chocolate: ¾ cup (127 g) white or milk chocolate, melted and cooled

Lemon: 2 tsp (10 g) lemon extract

Coconut: ⅓ cup (80 g) full fat coconut cream and 1 tsp coconut extract

Caramel: ½ cup (160 g) caramel

Peanut butter: ½ cup (125 g) smooth peanut butter

Chocolate-hazelnut: ½ cup (150 g) chocolate-hazelnut spread

The buttercream will become a lot softer after some of these additions. If you'd like a thicker consistency add ¼ cup (32 g) of powdered sugar and mix to combine. Continue adding until the preferred consistency is reached.

Decorating Tutorials

Ice Cream Soda Cupcakes

These have got to be some of the cutest cupcakes ever and so much fun to make. They look just like "spiders" (what us Aussies call ice cream sodas) down to the very last detail—only they don't melt!

Makes approximately 12 regular cupcakes

1 batch Pink Lemonade Cupcakes (page 72)

1 batch Fancy American Buttercream (page 76)

12 maraschino cherries

½ batch White Chocolate Ganache (page 29)

White gel food coloring

Electric/neon pink gel food coloring

Small angled offset spatula

Medium spring action round ice cream scoop

2 piping bags

Rainbow sprinkles

21 piping tip

Pink paper straws

1. Bake the pink lemonade cupcakes and set them aside to cool.

2. Prepare the buttercream. Remove approximately ½ cup (75 g) and set it aside. Chill the remaining buttercream in the fridge for 30 minutes.

3. Place the cherries on a paper towel to absorb the liquid and set them aside.

4. Once the cupcakes are cool and the buttercream is firm, prepare the ganache. Add 2 to 3 drops of white gel coloring and mix well to combine. Then add 2 to 3 drops of pink gel coloring and mix well to combine. Set aside to cool.

5. Use an offset spatula or knife to dab some of the room-temperature buttercream on top of each cupcake.

6. Use the ice cream scoop to make balls from the chilled buttercream, scraping along the side of the bowl so that the bottom of the ball is flat and sits flush on the cupcake. If the buttercream is still too soft, let it chill in the fridge until it's firm enough to scoop. Place a ball on top of each cupcake. The spring-action scoop will help the balls release easily and the dab of buttercream will help them stick to the tops of the cupcakes. If the ganache still hasn't cooled, chill the cupcakes in the fridge until it has.

7. Stir the cooled ganache to make it smooth and pour it into a piping bag. Twist the top of the bag and cut off the tip, approximately ¼ inch (0.5 cm).

8. For each cupcake, hold the bag just above the buttercream and apply gentle pressure until the ganache starts oozing out. Keeping the pressure even, move the tip of the bag around the top of the buttercream so that the ganache drips down all the sides.

9. Use a spoon to pour sprinkles onto the ganache drips and chill the cupcakes in the fridge for 5 minutes.

10. Fit a piping bag with the tip and fill it with the room-temperature buttercream using the method on page 36.

11. Remove the cupcakes from the fridge. For each cupcake, hold the piping bag directly over the ganache and apply gentle pressure until buttercream starts coming out, the same way as a soft serve ice cream machine. Once you've made a small dollop of buttercream, release pressure and pull up and away.

12. Place a cherry on top of each buttercream dollop.

13. Cut the straws into 2-inch (5-cm) pieces and stick them into the sides of each buttercream ball.

Cotton Candy Cupcakes

If you had to imagine what eating a cloud would be like, this would be it. The only thing better than sugar, is spun sugar. The way it melts in your mouth is just divine. Add it to a cupcake and . . . well, I'll just leave that mental image there. There's a bit of an art to eating this one. Refrain from picking off the cotton candy, eating it and then moving onto the cupcake. The buttercream nest is there for a purpose, not just to look good. The idea is to push the cotton candy into the nest, so that when you bite into the cupcake, you get a bit of everything. Did I just blow your mind?

Makes approximately 12 regular cupcakes ·

1 batch Pink Lemonade Cupcakes (page 72)

1 batch Fancy American Buttercream (page 76)

Electric/neon pink and blue gel food coloring

Piping bag

8B piping tip

Pink and blue sprinkle medley

Pink edible glitter

Pink and blue cotton candy

1. Bake the pink lemonade cupcakes and set them aside to cool.

2. Prepare the buttercream and divide it between two bowls. Add 3 to 4 drops of pink gel coloring to one and 3 to 4 drops of blue gel coloring to the other. Mix each one well to combine.

3. Fit the piping bag with the tip and fill one side with pink buttercream and the other side with blue, using the method on page 38.

4. Pipe a nest on top of each cupcake by starting in the middle and applying gentle pressure until buttercream starts coming out. Keeping the pressure even, slowly make a spiral around the top of the cupcake in a counterclockwise motion.

5. Once you reach the outer edge of the cupcake and have made a full rotation, continue to make another circle around the edge only. Once done, release pressure and pull away. This should make a "nest" with a space in the middle.

6. Pour the sprinkles and glitter over the buttercream.

7. Tear off pieces of cotton candy and place them in the nests, then sprinkle more glitter over the top.

Note

Serve these immediately, as cotton candy begins to dissolve once it makes contact with moisture. If you're making them for a later time, set the cupcakes aside in an airtight container and place the cotton candy on top just before serving.

Galaxy Cupcakes

The first time I made these was for my son who had a solid three-year obsession with the solar system. At the age of two, he knew the names of all the planets and their moons. He knew the attributes and size of each planet and would correct people when they referred to Pluto as a planet, as it's actually a dwarf planet (duh!). Anyway, of course he wanted a solar system themed 5th birthday, and I was happy to oblige. When presented with the solar system cupcakes, he asked where the planets were. I had learnt enough from him to be able to quickly reply that they'd been sucked into a black hole. He was satisfied with this answer and loved his cupcakes. Everyone loved his cupcakes. However, from then on, I dropped the title "solar system cupcakes" and they became "galaxy cupcakes."

Makes approximately 12 regular cupcakes ···

1 batch Chocolate-Hazelnut Cupcakes (page 75)

12 white chocolate stars (page 42 or 43)

2 paintbrushes

Edible glue

Silver edible glitter

1 batch white chocolate Fancy American Buttercream (page 76)

¼ cup (25 g) unsweetened cocoa powder

Super black gel food coloring

Electric/neon pink and blue gel food coloring

Piping bag

8B piping tip

Galaxy sprinkle medley

Silver edible stars

1. Bake the chocolate-hazelnut cupcakes and set them aside to cool.

2. Prepare the glitter white chocolate stars by using the first or second method on pages 42 and 43. Once set, use a paintbrush to cover the stars with a thin layer of edible glue. Then use the other paintbrush to paint on the glitter. Set them aside to dry.

3. Prepare the white chocolate buttercream and divide it among three bowls.

4. Add the cocoa to the first bowl and mix well to combine. Add 2 to 3 drops of black gel coloring and mix well to combine. Continue adding the black gel coloring 1 drop at a time and mixing well until the buttercream is black.

5. Add 2 to 3 drops of pink gel coloring to the second bowl and mix well to combine. Add 2 to 3 drops of blue gel coloring to the third bowl and mix well to combine.

6. Fit the piping bag with the tip and fill it with all three colored buttercreams using the method on page 38.

7. Pipe an ice cream swirl on top of each cupcake using the method on page 39.

8. Pour the sprinkles over the buttercream, followed by the stars and glitter.

9. Place a glitter white chocolate star on top of each cupcake.

Sprinkle Cupcakes

As far as trends go, the classic sprinkle cupcake will always be popular and a party favorite. I love the way some simple sprinkles add a new dimension and texture to an already delicious cupcake. The soft and moist base, paired with creamy buttercream and crunchy sprinkles, make for the perfect treat. Plus, they look so good and are super easy to make. They're just all-around winners.

Makes approximately 12 regular cupcakes ···

1 batch Coconut Cupcakes
(page 73)

12 pink chocolate hearts (page 43)

Rainbow sprinkle medley

1 batch lemon Fancy American
Buttercream (page 76)

Electric/neon pink gel food
coloring

Piping bag

1A piping tip

1. Bake the coconut cupcakes and set them aside to cool.

2. Make the pink chocolate sprinkle hearts using the second method on page 43. Once you've poured the chocolate onto the silicone mat or parchment paper and spread it out, cover it with sprinkles.

3. Prepare the lemon buttercream and color it with 4 to 5 drops of pink gel coloring. Mix well to combine.

4. Fit the piping bag with the tip and fill it with the buttercream using the method on page 36.

5. Pipe a bulb onto each cupcake using the method on page 39 and chill them in the fridge for 10 minutes.

6. Pour the sprinkles into a small bowl. Hold the cupcake upside down and gently place the buttercream bulb into the bowl of sprinkles, turning it around to ensure it is fully covered.

7. Once the pink chocolate sprinkle hearts have set, bury them slightly into the top of each cupcake.

Rainbow Cupcakes

Okay, this cupcake is so cute that you won't want to eat it. You will though, maybe even two. Or three. Rainbows make everyone smile, as do cupcakes, so it was only natural to combine the two. The only aversion I have to rainbows is the color red. I love it for clothing and lipstick, but that's about it. What I would really like to see is a rainbow with pink in it. In this case, it does.

Makes approximately 12 regular cupcakes ···

1 batch Vanilla Cupcakes (page 69)

Electric/neon pink, blue, yellow, orange and green gel food coloring

12 mini marble chocolate bars (page 42)

Pink, purple and green oil-based chocolate coloring gel or powder

Paintbrush

Pink luster dust

1 batch Fancy American Buttercream (page 76)

Piping bag

1A tip

Rainbow sprinkle medley

1. Prepare the batter for the vanilla cupcakes. Once the dry and wet ingredients are almost incorporated, divide the batter among five small bowls. Color each one individually with 2 to 3 drops of pink, blue, yellow, orange and green gel coloring. Mix each one until just combined and then spoon a small amount of each colored batter into the cupcake liners until they're two-thirds full. Bake the vanilla cupcakes according to the instructions and set them aside to cool.

2. Make the mini marble chocolate bars using the first method on page 42. Divide the chocolate among three small bowls and color each one individually with 1 to 2 drops of pink, purple and green chocolate coloring gel or a pinch of pink, purple and green chocolate coloring powder. Mix well to combine.

3. Use a spoon to drizzle lines of pink chocolate over the cavities, followed by purple and then green until they are full. Once set, use the paintbrush to powder luster dust over each one. Set them aside.

4. Prepare the buttercream and divide it among five bowls and color each one individually with 2 to 3 drops of pink, blue, yellow, orange and green gel coloring. Mix each one well to combine.

5. Fit the piping bag with the tip and fill it with all five colored buttercreams using the method on page 38.

6. Pipe an ice cream swirl on top of each cupcake using the method on page 39.

7. Use a spoon to pour sprinkles around the base of the swirl, then stick a mini marble chocolate bar in the top.

Note

Mini chocolate bar molds can be found online. If you're unable to acquire one, you can use a large store-bought white chocolate bar, break it into individual pieces and use the paintbrush to powder luster dust over each one.

Pink Marble Choc Top Cupcakes

Like sprinkles, chocolate makes everything even better. As a kid, I used to live for the sweet sound of the music coming from the ice cream truck, letting us know it was approaching. My ultimate favorite was a soft serve cone dipped in chocolate. This love for chocolate dipping extends much further than just ice cream though, and I'm pretty sure I'm not the only one. Seen the candy aisle at the supermarket lately? Everything is coated in milk or white chocolate, from licorice to pretzels to marshmallows. It had to be done with cupcakes, especially this one. Chocolate-hazelnut buttercream coated in white chocolate? Definitely.

Makes approximately 12 regular cupcakes

1 batch Vanilla Cupcakes (page 69)

12 mini pink chocolate bars (page 42)

1 batch chocolate-hazelnut Fancy American Buttercream (page 76)

Piping bag

1A piping tip

3 cups (510 g) white chocolate

¼ cup (60 g) vegetable oil

White and pink oil-based chocolate coloring gel or powder

Tall drinking glass (wide enough to dip a cupcake into)

Pink sprinkle medley

Note

You will not use all the chocolate, but there needs to be enough to dip and fully cover the buttercream swirl. The remaining chocolate can be used to make chocolate decorations, however the presence of cocoa butter from it being real chocolate as well as the added oil, will result in it taking longer to set. It can also be used to coat things like strawberries, cherries or marshmallows.

1. Bake the vanilla cupcakes and set them aside to cool.

2. Make the mini pink chocolate bars using the first method on page 42. Mini chocolate bar molds can be found online. If you're unable to acquire one, you can use a large store-bought white chocolate bar and break it into individual pieces. The white color will still match the marbling effect.

3. Prepare the chocolate-hazelnut buttercream.

4. Fit the piping bag with the tip and fill it with the buttercream using the method on page 36.

5. Pipe an ice cream swirl onto each cupcake using the method on page 39 and place the cupcakes in the freezer for 15 minutes.

6. Melt the chocolate and oil together in the microwave for 30 seconds, then in 15-second increments until it's just melted. Be careful not to overheat the chocolate, otherwise it won't set later. Mix well to make sure the oil and chocolate are incorporated.

7. Pour half the chocolate into another bowl. Color each one individually with 2 to 3 drops of white chocolate coloring gel or a pinch of white chocolate coloring powder and 2 to 3 drops of pink chocolate coloring gel or a pinch of pink chocolate coloring powder. Mix each one well to combine.

8. Pour half of the white chocolate and half of the pink chocolate into the glass and stir slightly to make a marbled effect.

9. Decorate the cupcakes one by one. Remove a cupcake from the freezer and dip it upside down into the chocolate until the buttercream is fully covered. Lift the cupcake out of the chocolate and twist the cupcake from left to right to allow the excess chocolate to drip off. Place the cupcake right side up.

10. Use a spoon to pour sprinkles around the base of the swirl and place a mini pink chocolate bar or white chocolate piece on top. As you decorate the remaining cupcakes, if the chocolate begins to blend, add a little more of each color to maintain the marble effect

11. Allow the chocolate to set before serving.

Candy Cupcakes

What is there to say about this? Other than it could also be called "trip-to-the-dentist cupcake"? Yes, it's a bit over-the-top, but this is my book, and I'll add candy if I want to. Don't knock it till you've tried it. Seriously though, these are ridiculously good, especially with sour candy or licorice on top. They cut down the sweetness and add a new element of flavor. It's pretty much a party in your mouth.

Makes approximately 12 regular cupcakes ···

1 batch Vanilla Cupcakes (page 69)

1 batch Fancy American Buttercream (page 76)

Electric/neon pink, purple, green and yellow gel food coloring

Piping bag

8B piping tip

Rainbow sprinkle medley

Small candy pieces (I have used licorice cubes, sprinkles-covered licorice, jellybeans and rainbow sour strips)

1. Bake the vanilla cupcakes and set them aside to cool.

2. Prepare the buttercream and divide it among four bowls. Color each one individually with 2 to 3 drops of pink, purple, green and yellow gel coloring. Mix each one well to combine.

3. Fit the piping bag with the tip and fill it with all four colored buttercreams using the method on page 38.

4. Pipe a swirl on top of each cupcake using the method on page 39.

5. Use a spoon to pour sprinkles over the buttercream.

6. Place the candy pieces on top of the buttercream starting with the largest, then the smallest to fill any gaps.

Neon Cupcakes

These cupcakes just scream fun. They have a definite '80s vibe to them, so being born in that decade, I had to include them. I want to love pastels and have tried to love them, but ultimately my heart belongs to the bright neon colors. Interestingly, there's a way to make cupcakes and other desserts glow, but it requires a lot of effort for something you're going to eat. At that point I'll just have a neon cupcake with a side of glowstick.

Makes approximately 12 regular cupcakes ···

1 batch Lemon Cupcakes (page 71)

Electric/neon yellow and green gel food coloring

36 neon orange chocolate shards (page 41)

1 batch Fancy American Buttercream (page 76)

Piping bag

1M piping tip

Silver edible glitter

Bright pink sprinkles

Pink metallic rods

1. Prepare the batter for the lemon cupcakes. Add 3 to 4 drops of yellow gel coloring to the wet ingredients. Mix well to combine before pouring the wet ingredients into the dry ingredients. Bake the lemon cupcakes according to the instructions and set them aside to cool.

2. Make the neon orange chocolate shards using the method on page 41. If you can't find neon orange chocolate coloring, regular orange is fine. Score the lines to make the shards small so that you will have 36 from one batch. Set them aside.

3. Make the buttercream and color it with 4 to 5 drops of green gel coloring. Mix well to combine.

4. Fit the piping bag with the tip and fill it with the buttercream using the method on page 36.

5. Pipe an ice cream swirl onto each cupcake using the method on page 39.

6. Use a spoon to pour glitter over the buttercream, followed by sprinkles. Place some metallic rods onto the buttercream and then stick in 3 neon orange chocolate shards.

Cookie Class

Cookies must be the most popular and timeless treats ever. I mean, Santa Claus, one of the most well-known figures in the entire world, prefers cookies on Christmas Eve over absolutely everything else. Need I say more? I've heard people say they don't like cake (these people are not my friends, FYI), but no one dislikes cookies. The great thing about them is that there are countless varieties, so everyone is sure to find one they love. Here in Australia, you aren't even an Aussie if a "cuppa and biccie" (cup of tea and biscuit) isn't practically your religion.

Just to touch on why cookies are so good and so loved—they're mostly sugar and butter, two of the best things ever. If stored correctly, they can last ages. They are fantastic for bribing children into behaving (some adults too, for that matter). They're quick to make and bake. You can sandwich ice cream, buttercream or basically any filling between two of them and make the world's best dessert. I'm quite certain that most people have a favorite go-to, foolproof cookie recipe. If you don't, look no further. If you do, here's your chance to add another one to your list or maybe discover something you didn't even know you were missing.

To put it simply, cookies are the leaders of the baking world. Other dessert trends will come and go, but cookies will stand the test of time. This chapter will cover a range of recipes from classic sugar cookies to more elaborate pinwheel cookie pops, and everything in between. The flavors and textures will vary between sweet, buttery, soft, crunchy and chewy—something to satisfy everyone. The decorating tutorials will put a spin on the more classic recipes, making them a bit more delicious and a lot more fun, easy to achieve but very effective at the same time. The days of simple or plain cookies are a thing of the past.

Sugar Cookies

Sugar cookies are where it all began for me (hence my business name Sugar & Salt Cookies). At the time, they were the only things I knew how to make well. I don't make them often these days, but when I do, it's a very nostalgic experience. Sugar cookies were my starting point. As bakers, we all need a starting point; something to master and to give us confidence before moving on to the next thing. If that's you, I really recommend these sugar cookies. If not . . . just make them anyway. They're so soft and tender, without being fragile, and have the most divine flavor of butter and vanilla. It's a win-win situation.

Makes approximately 30 cookies

3¼ cups (406 g) all-purpose flour

¾ tsp salt

1 cup (227 g) unsalted butter, softened

1 cup (200 g) caster sugar or superfine sugar

1 large egg

2 tsp (10 g) vanilla extract

Parchment paper

Rolling pin

Medium heart cookie cutter

In a medium bowl, whisk together the flour and salt. In the bowl of a stand mixer, cream the butter and sugar with the paddle attachment on medium-high speed until fluffy, approximately 2 minutes. Add the egg and vanilla and beat for another minute. Scrape down the sides of the bowl. Add the dry ingredients to the bowl and mix on low speed until combined.

Take half the dough and wrap in plastic wrap. Flatten it with the palm of your hand to make a disc approximately 1 inch (2.5 cm) thick. Repeat with the remaining dough. Chill the dough in the fridge for 1 hour.

Remove one disc of dough from the plastic wrap and place it on a cutting board covered with a sheet of parchment paper. Roll it out with a rolling pin until it's approximately ¼ inch (0.5 cm) thick and then place the board in the fridge to chill the dough for 15 minutes. Repeat with the other half of wrapped dough.

Remove one sheet of chilled dough from the fridge and use a cookie cutter to cut out the hearts. Place the hearts on a baking tray lined with parchment paper and place it in the freezer for 30 minutes.

Preheat the oven to 355°F (180°C).

Remove the tray from the freezer and place it immediately in the oven. Bake on the middle rack for 8 minutes or until the edges just begin to turn golden brown, rotating halfway through. While they are baking, repeat the process with the second sheet of chilled dough.

Allow the cookies to cool for 10 minutes on the baking tray before transferring them to a wire rack to cool completely.

Sprinkle and White Choc Chip Cookies

What we have here is the queen of all cookies. Chunky, chewy, soft and stuffed with all the sprinkles and white chocolate chips your heart desires. These are my ultimate weakness and I would happily let them ruin my appetite anytime. In fact, they're so tempting even to look at, that a girl I know gobbled one up despite being gluten-intolerant and knowing she may have been in for a rough night. She had no regrets.

Makes approximately 20 cookies

3 cups (375 g) all-purpose flour

1 tbsp (10 g) cornflour (or cornstarch)

1½ tsp (6 g) baking powder

½ tsp baking soda

¾ tsp salt

1 cup (227 g) unsalted butter, melted and cooled

1⅔ cups (330 g) sugar

2 large eggs

1 tbsp (15 g) vanilla extract

1 cup (170 g) white chocolate chips

¼ cup (50 g) rainbow sprinkles

In a medium bowl, whisk together the flour, cornflour, baking powder, baking soda and salt. In a large bowl, whisk together the melted butter and sugar until combined. Add the eggs and vanilla and whisk to combine. Add the dry ingredients to the wet and mix until combined. Pour in the white chocolate chips and sprinkles and give it one last mix. Cover the bowl with plastic wrap and chill the dough in the fridge for at least 1 hour.

Preheat the oven to 350°F (175°C) and line a baking tray with parchment paper.

Once the dough is chilled, use an ice cream scoop to make dough balls, about 2½ tablespoons (60 g) each, and place them 4 inches (10 cm) apart. Place the remaining dough in the fridge until you're ready to bake another tray.

Bake on the middle rack for 11 minutes, rotating the tray halfway through. The cookies will seem slightly underdone but will continue to bake on the tray once removed from the oven. This is how they turn out soft and chewy. Allow the cookies to cool completely on the baking tray.

Notes

For very thick cookies, add an extra 3 tablespoons (25 g) of flour.

For flatter cookies, press down gently on them once they've been removed from the oven or remove 3 tablespoons (25 g) of flour from the recipe. For crispy edges, roll the dough balls so that they are taller than they are wide.

Decorating Tutorials

Rainbow Butter Cookies

When I hear "butter" and "rainbow" in the same sentence, my heart starts beating at an abnormally high rate. Before you start googling the difference between sugar and butter cookies, let me explain. Sugar cookies have a similar ratio of sugar to butter. Butter cookies have a much higher ratio of butter to sugar. Not exactly rocket science, but there you have it. Due to the higher butter content, these cookies literally melt in your mouth. The added bonus is that these are dipped in pink chocolate..

Makes approximately 24 cookies ···

2 cups (250 g) all-purpose flour

3 tbsp (30 g) cornflour (or cornstarch)

½ tsp salt

1 cup (227 g) unsalted butter, softened

⅔ cup (83 g) powdered sugar

1 large egg

2 tsp (10 g) vanilla extract

Electric/neon pink, blue, yellow and orange gel food coloring

Piping bag

Large open star piping tip (Ateco 827, Wilton 8B or anything equivalent)

1 cup (170 g) white chocolate

Pink chocolate coloring gel or powder

Rainbow sprinkle medley

1. In a medium bowl, whisk together the flour, cornflour and salt. In the bowl of a stand mixer, cream the butter and sugar with the paddle attachment on medium-high speed until fluffy, approximately 2 minutes. Add the egg and vanilla extract and beat for another minute. The mixture will look curdled. Scrape down the sides of the bowl. Pour the dry ingredients into the bowl and mix on low speed until combined. The batter should be smooth enough that you can pipe with it. Divide the batter among four small bowls and color each one individually with 2 drops of pink, blue, yellow and orange gel food coloring. Mix each one well to combine.

2. Fit the piping bag with the tip and fill it with all four colored batters using the method on page 38. On a baking tray lined with parchment paper, pipe cookies into little swirls using the method on page 39. Place the tray in the freezer for 1 hour. Preheat the oven to 375°F (190°C). Remove the tray from the freezer and place it immediately in the oven. Bake on the middle rack for 10 minutes, rotating halfway through. Allow the cookies to cool for 10 minutes on the baking tray before transferring them to a wire rack to cool completely.

3. Heat the chocolate in the microwave for 30 seconds, then in 15-second increments until it's melted. Be careful not to overheat the chocolate, otherwise it won't set later. Add 2 to 3 drops of pink chocolate coloring gel or a pinch of pink chocolate coloring powder and mix well to combine. Dip the cooled cookies into the chocolate so they are approximately one-third coated. Shake the cookie gently to make any excess chocolate drip off. Lay the cookie on a sheet of parchment paper or a wire rack, and use a spoon to pour sprinkles over the chocolate.

Notes

If the batter is too thick to pipe, roll the bag between your hands for 1 to 2 minutes to warm it up and soften it.

If the parchment paper moves while you're piping, transfer it to a cutting board. Use clothespins to secure the parchment paper to the board so it doesn't move while you pipe.

Marble Cookies

Marble cookies were my breakthrough in the baking world. I'd been inspired to make them after receiving some beautiful marble chocolates. I love how the marble adds an elegant touch to an otherwise simple sugar cookie, and how each one is unique with its marbling. The possibilities are endless when it comes to colors too, so there's lots of fun experimenting to be had while making these.

Makes approximately 30 cookies ....

1 batch Sugar Cookies (page 98)

1 (17.5-oz [500-g]) package white fondant

Electric/neon pink gel food coloring

Rolling pin

Parchment paper

Medium heart cookie cutter

2 paintbrushes

Edible metallic pink paint

1. Bake the sugar cookies and set them aside to cool.

2. Tear off approximately 3.5 ounces (100 g) of fondant, add 2 to 3 drops of pink gel coloring to it, and roll it in your hands until the color has combined.

3. With clean hands, knead the remaining white fondant into a large ball.

4. Divide the pink fondant into 7 or 8 pieces and then squash them separately into the large white fondant ball.

5. Twist the fondant in different directions so that the pink spreads and makes a marbled effect. Do not mix too much or the marbled effect will be less obvious.

6. Roll out the fondant onto a sheet of parchment paper with the rolling pin until it's approximately $1/16$ inch (2 mm) thick.

7. Use the cookie cutter to cut out hearts and then pull away the leftover fondant. Repeat with the remaining fondant until you have enough hearts for all the cookies. Allow the hearts to dry out for 10 minutes so that they're easier to handle.

8. Use a paintbrush to brush a cookie lightly with water and then place a fondant heart gently on top. Repeat with the remaining cookies.

9. Dip the other paintbrush into the edible pink paint and splatter it over the cookies by tapping the paintbrush against your finger.

Watercolor Cookies

These cookies are just the prettiest things. The painted watercolor effect on white fondant is so beautiful, and I will take any excuse to not roll color into fondant and end up with pink hands for the rest of the week. The watercolor "paint" comes from mixing food gel coloring with rose spirit or vodka. Before you get excited about the use of vodka, let me just warn you that it evaporates immediately; that's what makes it the magic ingredient. If you used water instead, the color would never dry. So no, you're not getting tipsy from these, not even close. This is a PG-rated cookbook!

Makes approximately 30 cookies ···

1 batch Sugar Cookies (page 98)

1 (17.5-oz [500-g]) package white fondant

Rolling pin

Parchment paper

Medium heart cookie cutter

4 paintbrushes

2 tbsp (30 g) rose spirit or clear vodka

Electric/neon yellow, pink and purple gel food coloring

Pink edible glitter

1. Bake the sugar cookies and set them aside to cool.

2. Knead the fondant into a ball and roll it on a sheet of parchment paper with the rolling pin until it's approximately 1/16 inch (2 mm) thick.

3. Use the cookie cutter to cut out hearts and then pull away the leftover fondant. Repeat with the remaining fondant until you have enough hearts for all the cookies. Allow the hearts to dry out for 10 minutes so that they're easier to handle

4. Use a paintbrush to brush a cookie lightly with water and then place a fondant heart gently on top. Repeat with the remaining cookies.

5. Take three small cups and pour 2 teaspoons (10 g) of rose spirit or clear vodka into each. Color each one individually by using toothpicks to dab in a tiny bit of the yellow, pink and purple gel colorings. Stir each one with a separate paintbrush to combine.

6. Use the paintbrushes to paint or smear the colors over the fondant, allowing them to blend slightly with each other. For a stronger color, add a little more gel coloring. For a more diluted color, add a little more rose spirit or vodka.

7. Sprinkle glitter over the cookies before the "paint" dries.

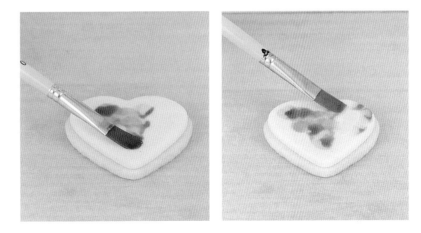

Buttercream Swirl Cookies

For those of you who aren't too big on fondant, I haven't forgotten about you. I'm considerate like that. What we have here is a delicious sugar cookie base with a creamy buttercream topping. Not just smeared-on buttercream either, but swirly buttercream covered in edible glitter and stars for your aesthetic pleasure too. We're fancy in this book.

Makes approximately 30 cookies

1 batch Sugar Cookies (page 98)

1 batch lemon Fancy American Buttercream (page 76)

Electric/neon pink, purple, yellow and orange gel food coloring

2 piping bags

21 and 199 piping tips

Gold edible stars

Gold edible glitter

1. Bake the sugar cookies and set them aside to cool.

2. Prepare the lemon buttercream and divide it among four bowls. Color each one individually with 2 to 3 drops of pink, purple, yellow and orange gel coloring. Mix each one well to combine.

3. Fit a piping bag with the 21 tip and fill it with pink and orange buttercream using the method on page 38.

4. Fit the other piping bag with the 199 tip and fill it with purple and yellow buttercream using the method on page 38.

5. Use the 21 tip to pipe 3 or 4 swirls over the cookies using the method on page 39.

6. Use both the 21 and 199 tips to pipe stars to fill in the gaps using the method on page 39.

7. Use a spoon to sprinkle the stars and glitter over each cookie.

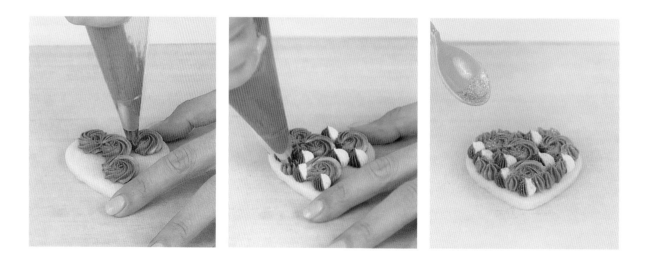

Sweet Sandwiches

One thing people always ask me is if I'm constantly stuffing my face with cake. The answer is no (unless I'm testing a recipe, which is quite often. So actually, yes, I am). When you're around as much cake as me, the novelty of eating it does wear off after a while though. You sort of have to be in the mood. Well, these cookie sandwiches are the exception. They are SO good. One time I was due to have quite major surgery. I noticed some missed calls from my family and figured they had called to wish me luck. Turns out they just wanted to know if I had time to make a batch of these before heading to the hospital. Cookie sandwich: 1, Me: 0.

Makes approximately 10 sandwiches ······································

1 batch Sprinkle and White Choc Chip Cookies (page 99)

½ batch Fancy American Buttercream (page 76)

Electric/neon pink gel food coloring

2 piping bags

1M piping tip

Filling such as chocolate-hazelnut spread, caramel (page 138) or peanut butter (optional)

Rainbow sprinkle medley

1. Bake the cookies and set them aside to cool.

2. Prepare the buttercream and color it with 3 to 4 drops of pink gel coloring. Mix well to combine.

3. Fit the piping bag with the tip and fill it with buttercream using the method on page 36.

4. With the bottom side facing up, pipe a swirl onto half of the cookies using the method on page 39.

5. If you would like an added filling, then microwave your choice in increments of 10 seconds until it's smooth but not runny. If you are using the caramel from this book, it will not need to be softened.

6. Pour the filling into another piping bag and cut off the tip, about ¼ inch (0.5 cm).

7. Drizzle the filling over the buttercream, then place another cookie on top right side up. Gently press down so everything is stuck together.

8. Spoon sprinkles onto the buttercream around the sides of the cookie sandwiches.

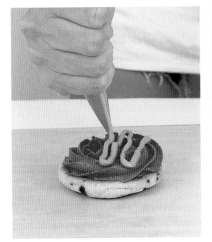

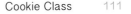

Pinwheel Cookie Pops

I love when kids are presented with these. They are always mesmerized. Is it a cookie? Is it a lollipop? Do you lick it? Can I have five? My daughter has an insane sweet tooth (surprised?) and her favorite things are cookies and lollipops. Whenever she was rewarded with a treat, she'd be divided between the two and would obviously attempt to convince me to give her both. No such luck, despite some very impressive efforts for a three-year-old. Then the cookie pop came into our lives and we've never looked back.

Makes approximately 24 cookie pops

2½ cups (312 g) all-purpose flour

2 tbsp (20 g) cornflour (or cornstarch)

¾ tsp salt

¾ cup (170 g) unsalted butter, softened

¾ cup (150 g) caster sugar or superfine sugar

1 large egg

2 tsp (10 g) vanilla extract

Electric/neon pink and blue gel food coloring

Oven-safe lollipop sticks

1. In a medium bowl, whisk together the flour, cornflour and salt.

2. In the bowl of a stand mixer, cream the butter and sugar with the paddle attachment on medium-high speed until fluffy, approximately 2 minutes.

3. Add the egg and vanilla extract and beat for another minute. Scrape down the sides of the bowl.

4. Add the dry ingredients to the bowl and mix on low speed until just combined.

5. Take half the dough and color it with 2 to 3 drops of pink gel coloring. Knead it well to combine. Wrap the dough in plastic wrap and place it in the fridge to chill for 1 hour.

6. Repeat with the blue gel coloring for the other half.

7. Remove all the dough from the fridge. Make small balls of each colored dough, approximately ½ tablespoon (12 g) each in size.

8. Take one ball of pink dough and on a sheet of parchment paper roll it out into a rope approximately 6 inches (15 cm) in length. Repeat with a ball of blue dough.

9. Place the two ropes next to each other and gently twist them together. Once twisted together, roll gently so the rope is smooth, but the colors are still separate.

10. Place the rope on a tray lined with parchment paper and curl it into a pinwheel.

11. Insert the lollipop stick into the bottom of the wheel. Repeat with the remaining dough balls and chill them in the freezer for 30 minutes. (You will have two to three trays.)

12. Preheat the oven to 355°F (180°C).

13. Remove one tray at a time from the freezer and place it immediately in the oven. Bake on the middle rack for 10 minutes, rotating halfway through.

14. Allow the cookies to cool for 10 minutes on the baking tray before transferring them to a wire rack to cool completely.

Tempting Treats

Don't be fooled into thinking that this chapter is less important just because it's last. We all know how often the best is saved for last, and let me tell you, some of these recipes have been more popular with my customers than anything else. In fact, I could almost bet that most people are skipping forward to read this chapter before anything else. These are the recipes I get asked about most.

These desserts are very nontraditional and probably where I've had the most fun experimenting and decorating. They all make great additions to a dessert table when you don't want cake to be the only option. I like to think of them as my "extra" desserts. Not extra as in leftovers. I mean extra as in FABULOUS.

For me, baking should be fun and make me happy. The recipes and tutorials in this chapter are relatively simple to navigate, so relax, turn your phone to "airplane" mode, put your headphones in and just have a good time with them.

Once you've had a go at my tutorials, you'll be able to let your imagination run wild with creativity. You can experiment with colors and toppings and piping methods—the options really are endless. For example, one of my favorite things is to pipe buttercream onto tarts and donuts for a little something different. It looks so good, and extra buttercream? Yes please. Some people might tell you that buttercream doesn't belong on tarts and donuts but ignore them. You really don't need that negativity in your life.

Vanilla Baked Donuts

The baked or "cake" donut has really taken off over the last few years, yet a lot of people are really divided when it comes to the comparison between them and the traditional fried donut. For me, there is no comparison. They are two completely different things with different ingredients, and I love them both equally. I chose to work with baked donuts for a few reasons though. The first being that they have a smooth surface, making them a dream to decorate. If you've ever tried glazing a lumpy fried donut, you'll know what I mean. The second is that they last longer than fried donuts, which dry out quite quickly. If you're a talented dessert eater like me and can finish a batch of fried donuts over the space of 24 hours, then that's great. If not, baked donuts are the perfect alternative. The final reason is that they're easier and quicker to make, which is essential when doing a big batch. I made 150 for a wedding once. It took all day, but the fried ones I probably would have finished about a week after the wedding was already over. Nothing like no dessert to ruin a wedding day.

Makes approximately 12 donuts

1¾ cups (219 g) all-purpose flour

1½ tsp (6 g) baking powder

¾ tsp salt

¼ cup (56 g) unsalted butter, melted and cooled

⅔ cup (130 g) caster sugar or superfine sugar

1 large egg, plus 1 yolk

⅔ cup (160 g) full fat milk

1 tbsp (15 g) vanilla extract

12-hole nonstick donut pan, approximately 3-inch (7-cm) cavities

Preheat the oven to 350°F (175°C).

In a large bowl, whisk together the flour, baking powder and salt. In a medium bowl, whisk together the butter and sugar. Add the egg, egg yolk, milk and vanilla extract and whisk again to combine. Add the wet ingredients to the dry and whisk until just combined. Do not overmix.

Spray the donut pan with nonstick cooking spray or grease each cavity with butter or vegetable oil. Use an ice cream scoop or spoon to fill the cavities halfway with batter. Place the tray in the oven on the middle rack and bake for 10 minutes, rotating halfway through.

Remove the tray from the oven and allow the donuts to cool completely before gently twisting them out of the cavities. Store them in an airtight container in the freezer overnight or at least a few hours until they're frozen, as this is how they need to be before glazing.

Cinnamon Baked Donuts

Hot cinnamon donuts are one of the best things ever. If you brought them to a dinner party, I'm pretty sure everyone would appreciate them more than any other fancy dessert. The cinnamon flavor is just right without being overpowering, and they don't have that oily feel that fried donuts sometimes have. Being baked, they're also slightly better for you than fried ones, so you can have two.

Makes approximately 12 donuts ....

1¾ cups (219 g) all-purpose flour

1½ tsp (6 g) baking powder

¾ tsp salt

½ tsp ground cinnamon

¼ cup (56 g) unsalted butter, melted and cooled

⅔ cup (130 g) caster sugar or superfine sugar

1 large egg, plus 1 yolk

⅔ cup (160 g) full fat milk

1 tbsp (15 g) vanilla extract

12-hole nonstick donut pan, approximately 3-inch (7-cm) cavities

CINNAMON TOPPING

½ cup (100 g) sugar

1 tsp ground cinnamon

¼ cup (56 g) unsalted butter, melted

Preheat the oven to 350°F (175°C).

In a large bowl, whisk together the flour, baking powder, salt and cinnamon. In a medium bowl, whisk together the butter and sugar. Add the egg, egg yolk, milk and vanilla extract and whisk again to combine. Add the wet ingredients to the dry and whisk until just combined. Do not overmix.

Spray the donut pan with nonstick cooking spray or grease each cavity with butter or vegetable oil. Use an ice cream scoop or spoon to fill the cavities halfway with batter. Place the tray in the oven on the middle rack and bake for 10 minutes, rotating halfway through.

Remove the tray from the oven and allow the donuts to cool completely before gently twisting them out of the cavities. To make the topping, place the sugar and cinnamon in a bowl and mix to combine. Dip the top of each donut into the bowl of melted butter and then into the cinnamon-sugar mixture.

Pink Lemonade Baked Donuts

I used to color my vanilla donuts pink, because I have an unhealthy obsession with that color. I just wanted everything to be pink. This didn't sit well with some people. It confused them. Vanilla baked goods were meant to be white or yellow. I was officially in trouble with the dessert color police! This turned out to be not a bad thing though, because then the pink lemonade donut was introduced and everything in the world made sense again.

Makes approximately 12 donuts ·

1¾ cups (219 g) all-purpose flour

1½ tsp (6 g) baking powder

¾ tsp salt

¼ cup (56 g) unsalted butter, melted and cooled

⅔ cup (130 g) caster sugar or superfine sugar

1 large egg, plus 1 yolk

⅔ cup (160 g) full fat milk

½ tbsp (7.5 g) lemon extract

½ tsp cotton candy flavoring

Electric/neon pink gel food coloring

12-hole nonstick donut pan, approximately 3-inch (7-cm) cavities

Preheat the oven to 350°F (175°C).

In a large bowl, whisk together the flour, baking powder and salt. In a medium bowl, whisk together the butter and sugar. Add the egg, egg yolk, milk, lemon extract, cotton candy flavoring and 2 to 3 drops of pink gel coloring and whisk again to combine. Add the wet ingredients to the dry and whisk until just combined. Do not overmix.

Spray the donut pan with nonstick cooking spray or grease each cavity with butter or vegetable oil. Use an ice cream scoop or spoon to fill the cavities halfway with batter. Place the tray in the oven on the middle rack and bake for 10 minutes, rotating halfway through.

Remove the tray from the oven and allow the donuts to cool completely before gently twisting them out of the cavities. Store them in an airtight container in the freezer overnight or at least a few hours until they're frozen, as this is how they need to be before glazing.

Lemon Rainbow Baked Donuts

There are two things in this world that possibly look better naked than dressed. Brad Pitt and these donuts. As far as "naked" donuts go, they don't get prettier than this. It's a struggle to glaze them and cover those beautiful bright colors. They are a little more time-consuming to make, but the end result is so worth it. Also, a photo of them makes the best phone screensaver.

Makes approximately 12 donuts

1¾ cups (219 g) all-purpose flour

1½ tsp (6 g) baking powder

¾ tsp salt

¼ cup (56 g) unsalted butter, melted and cooled

⅔ cup (130 g) caster sugar or superfine sugar

1 large egg, plus 1 yolk

⅔ cup (160 g) full fat milk

1 tbsp (15 g) lemon extract

Electric/neon pink, blue, purple, orange, yellow and green gel food coloring

12-hole nonstick donut pan, approximately 3-inch (7-cm) cavities

Preheat the oven to 350°F (175°C).

In a large bowl, whisk together the flour, baking powder and salt. In a medium bowl, whisk together the butter and sugar. Add the egg, egg yolk, milk and lemon extract and whisk again to combine. Add the wet ingredients to the dry and whisk until just combined. Separate the batter into six bowls and color each one individually with 2 drops of pink, blue, purple, orange, yellow and green gel coloring. Mix each one until just combined. Do not overmix.

Spray the donut tin with nonstick cooking spray or grease each cavity with butter or vegetable oil. Use an ice cream scoop or spoon to fill each cavity with a small amount of pink batter. Repeat with the blue batter and then purple, orange, yellow and green. Continue adding batter until the cavities are half-filled. Place the tray in the oven on the middle rack and bake for 10 minutes, rotating halfway through.

Remove the tray from the oven and allow the donuts to cool completely before gently twisting them out of the cavities. Store them in an airtight container in the freezer overnight or at least a few hours until they're frozen, as this is how they need to be before glazing.

Note

All donuts, whether plain or glazed, can be eaten chilled for a firmer texture or at room temperature for a softer texture.

Decorating Tutorials

Glitter Donuts

These babies here go through a three-stage process and people are majorly divided when it comes to which is the best. They start out as "naked" lemon rainbow donuts and are already so bright and fun. Then they're coated in a translucent glaze, which makes them so shiny and glossy (my favorite). Lastly, they're dusted with edible glitter because who wouldn't want to eat a glitter donut? Whichever stage you prefer, these donuts are without a doubt going to have a major "wow" factor—to look at AND to eat.

Makes approximately 12 donuts ....

1 batch Lemon Rainbow Baked Donuts (page 121)

1⅓ cups (166 g) powdered sugar

2 tsp (7 g) cornflour (or cornstarch)

2½ tbsp (37 g) water

Glitter dusting pump (optional)

Paintbrush

Silver edible glitter

1. Bake the lemon rainbow donuts. Once completely cooled, place them in an airtight container in the freezer overnight or for a few hours until they're frozen. Cold donuts make the glaze dry quicker without dripping.

2. Make the glaze by whisking together the powdered sugar, cornflour and water until it's smooth with no lumps.

3. Heat the glaze in the microwave for 10 seconds.

4. Remove the donuts from the freezer one at a time. Dip the top of the donut into the glaze and gently shake it to allow any excess to drip off. Place the donut right side up on a wire rack. The glaze is best warm for coating, so reheat it for 10 seconds after every three or four donuts.

5. Once all the donuts have been glazed, place them in the fridge to chill for 5 minutes. If your kitchen is warm, then place each donut immediately into the fridge once glazed, before glazing the next.

6. Use the dusting pump filled with glitter to spray glitter over the glaze, or a paintbrush to gently brush the glitter over the glaze. The donuts will no longer be frozen by this point, so they can be eaten immediately.

Notes

These measurements need to be very precise. If you accidentally add too much of something, even by the smallest amount, it may affect the consistency, shine and translucence of the glaze.

If the glaze drips too much, run your finger along the sides of the donuts to tidy them up.

If you want a thicker glaze you can add more powdered sugar, 1 teaspoon at a time, mixing well between each addition until the preferred consistency is reached. This will make the glaze more white and less translucent. Alternatively, chill the donuts for 5 minutes and coat them with a second layer of glaze.

Sprinkle Donuts

If you think of sprinkle donuts and Homer Simpson doesn't automatically come to mind, you've been hiding under a rock for 30 years. He made the sprinkle donut famous and for good reason. It's basically happiness with a hole in the middle. I love the classic look of a pink glaze covered in rainbow sprinkles, but sometimes when I feel like living on the edge, I use a mix of different sprinkles.

Makes approximately 12 donuts

1 batch Vanilla Baked Donuts
(page 116)

1 batch White Chocolate Ganache
(page 29)

White gel food coloring

Electric/neon pink gel food coloring

Rainbow sprinkles

Silver edible stars

Blue nonpareils

Orange/peach sanding sugar

Multicolored metallic rods

1. Bake the vanilla donuts. Once completely cooled, place them in an airtight container in the freezer overnight or for a few hours until they're frozen. Cold donuts make the glaze dry quicker without dripping.

2. Prepare the ganache. Add 2 to 3 drops of white gel coloring and mix well to combine, then add 2 to 3 drops of pink gel coloring and mix well to combine.

3. Remove the donuts from the freezer one at a time. Dip the top of the donut into the ganache and gently shake it to allow any excess to drip off. Place the donut right side up on a wire rack.

4. Use a spoon to pour one type of sprinkles over a small section of each donut, then repeat with the other sprinkle types one by one until the entire donut is covered.

Note

To avoid air bubbles in the ganache, stir it gently before dipping each donut.

Marble Donuts

I'll take any excuse to use a marbled decorating effect, so donuts were an absolute given. "More is more" applies to about 99 percent of the decorating tutorials in this book, but in this case less is definitely the way to go in order to appreciate the beautiful effect. I learned the hard way though. If there were such thing as Sprinkles Anonymous to treat the overuse of sprinkles, I would have been a regular. Marble donuts taught me to control my urge and to know when to put down the bottle—of sprinkles.

Makes approximately 12 donuts ···

1 batch Pink Lemonade Baked Donuts (page 118)

1 batch White Chocolate Ganache (page 29)

White gel food coloring

Electric/neon pink and yellow gel food coloring

Note

To avoid air bubbles in the ganache, stir it gently before dipping each donut, taking care to not blend the colors too much.

1. Bake the pink lemonade donuts. Once completely cooled, place them in an airtight container in the freezer overnight or for a few hours until they're frozen. Cold donuts make the glaze dry quicker without dripping.

2. Prepare the ganache. Add 2 to 3 drops of white gel coloring and mix well to combine. Divide the ganache between two bowls and color each one individually with 2 to 3 drops of pink and yellow gel coloring. Mix each one well to combine.

3. Drizzle half the yellow ganache over the pink and mix gently to make a marbled effect. Do not overmix or the colors will blend.

4. Remove the donuts from the freezer one at a time. Dip the top of the donut into the ganache and gently shake it to allow any excess to drip off. Place the donut right side up on a wire rack.

5. Once the colors start blending too much, drizzle the remaining yellow ganache into the bowl and mix very gently.

Colored Choc Drizzle Donuts

I love going to town on these donuts. I decided to use this decorating method a long time ago to cover some flaws in one of my first batches of donuts. I wasn't born a naturally talented donut glazer. Anyway, they looked so good and everyone loved them, so they ended up making regular appearances. Plus, chocolate squiggling is just FUN; I donut care how old or mature you are. (Sorry, I had to.)

Makes approximately 12 donuts ···

1 batch Cinnamon Baked Donuts
(page 117)

1 cup (170 g) white chocolate

Pink, orange and green oil-based
chocolate coloring gel or powder

3 piping bags

Rainbow sprinkle medley

1. Bake the cinnamon donuts and set them aside to cool.

2. Melt the chocolate in the microwave for 30 seconds, then in 15-second increments until it's melted. Be careful not to overheat the chocolate, otherwise it won't set later.

3. Divide the chocolate among three bowls and color each one individually with 2 drops of pink, orange and green chocolate coloring gel or a pinch of pink, orange and green chocolate coloring powder. Mix each one well to combine.

4. Pour the three colored chocolates into three separate piping bags.

5. Cut the tip off one piping bag, approximately ⅛ inch (3 mm), and drizzle the chocolate over each donut. Repeat with the remaining two colors, one at a time.

6. Use a spoon to pour the sprinkles over the chocolate drizzle before it sets.

Candy Cake Cones

There was a time when I was making so many cake cones that I honestly wondered if I would ever do anything else again. They are addictive to make, decorate and of course, eat. Plus, they're just as easy to make as cupcakes. I was utterly fascinated with slicing them open just to see the cone filled with cake. If there is one thing I love more than decorating and eating desserts then cutting them open would be it. I know I'm not the only one either, because there are thousands of videos on Instagram of it being done and people go crazy for them. I even went to the extent of buying fancy knives just to have that clean sharp cut. I will admit, my husband was slightly concerned for a while and may have slept with one eye open until the obsession wore off. They were some fun times.

Makes 12 cake cones

12 flat-bottomed wafer cones

Cone baking rack (optional)

1 batch Vanilla Cupcakes batter (page 69)

Electric/neon pink, blue, green, yellow and orange gel food coloring

1 batch Fancy American Buttercream (page 76)

Piping bag

1M piping tip

Rainbow sprinkle medley

Candy pieces (I have used sherbet saucers, rainbow twists, jellybeans and ice cream gummies)

Note

The moisture from the cupcake will eventually soften the cone. Store them in the fridge until they're ready to be served, to ensure the cone remains crisp.

1. Preheat the oven to 300°F (150°C).

2. Place the cones into the cone baking rack if you have one, or into the cavities of a cupcake pan.

3. Prepare the batter for the vanilla cupcakes. Once the dry and wet ingredients are almost incorporated, divide the batter among five small bowls. Color each one individually with 2 to 3 drops of pink, blue, green, yellow and orange gel coloring. Mix each one until just combined and then spoon a small amount of each colored batter into the cones until they're two-thirds full.

4. Place the cone baking rack in the oven on the level one below the middle and bake for 30 minutes, rotating the rack halfway through. If you're using a cupcake tin, place it in the oven carefully to ensure the cones don't fall.

5. After you remove the cones from the oven, immediately poke a hole in the bottom of each one with a skewer and transfer them to a wire rack to cool completely.

6. Prepare the buttercream and divide it among five bowls. Color each one individually with 2 to 3 drops of pink, blue, green, yellow and orange gel coloring. Mix each one well to combine.

7. Fit the piping bag with the tip and fill it with all five colored buttercreams using the method on page 38.

8. Pipe an ice cream swirl on top of each cupcake using the method on page 39.

9. Use a spoon to pour sprinkles over the buttercream.

10. Place the candy pieces on top of the buttercream starting with the largest, then the smallest to fill any gaps.

Pretty-in-Pink Cake Cones

I was out once with pink hair, nails, clothes and lipstick, and a friend said I looked like one of my desserts. While I make a lot of pink desserts, I didn't have anything that was exclusively pink, so naturally, it had to be done. One of my favorite sayings is "Pink makes me happy when I'm blue." Yes it does. So do these.

Makes 12 cake cones ···

1 batch Pink Lemonade Cupcakes (page 72)

12 mini pink chocolate bars (page 42)

Paintbrush

Pink luster dust

24 pink chocolate shards (page 41)

⅔ cup (112 g) white chocolate

Pink chocolate coloring gel or powder

12 waffle ice cream cones (pointed bottom)

Parchment paper

Pink sprinkle medley

¼ batch White Chocolate Ganache (page 29)

1 batch Fancy American Buttercream (page 76)

Electric/neon pink gel food coloring

Piping bag

1M piping tip

Pink metallic rods and candy pieces

Notes

The moisture from the cake balls will eventually soften the cone. Store them in the fridge to ensure the cone remains crisp.

If you don't have an ice cream cone holder, you can use a cardboard box or upside down egg carton. Simply cut small holes through either and place the cones inside.

1. Bake the pink lemonade cupcakes and set them aside to cool.

2. Make the mini pink chocolate bars using the first method on page 42. Once set, use the paintbrush to powder luster dust over each one. Mini chocolate bar molds can be found online. If you're unable to acquire one, you can use a large store-bought white chocolate bar, break it into individual pieces and use the paintbrush to powder luster dust over each one.

3. Make the pink chocolate shards using the method on page 41. Set all the pink chocolate shapes aside.

4. Heat the chocolate in a small bowl in the microwave for 30 seconds, then in 15-second increments until it's melted. Be careful not to overheat the chocolate, otherwise it won't set later. Add 2 to 3 drops of pink chocolate coloring gel or a pinch of pink chocolate coloring powder and mix well to combine.

5. Dip the rim of an ice cream cone into the chocolate and allow the excess to drip off. Place it on some parchment paper (pointed end up) and use a spoon to cover the chocolate with sprinkles. Allowing the chocolate to set slightly first will prevent the sprinkles from dripping. The chocolate should be soft, but not runny. Repeat with the remaining cones and set them aside.

6. Once the cupcakes have completely cooled, remove them from their liners and place them in a large bowl. Use your hands to pull them apart.

7. Make the ganache and pour it over the crumbled cupcakes. Use your hands to mix everything together, then make 12 balls approximately 2 tablespoons (50 g) each in size. Set them aside.

8. Once the cones have set, gently press a cake ball into each one. Set them aside.

9. Make the buttercream and color it with 3 to 4 drops of pink gel coloring. Mix well to combine.

10. Fit the piping bag with the tip and fill it with the buttercream using the method on page 36. Pipe an ice cream swirl on top of each cone using the method on page 39.

11. Place two pink chocolate shards and a mini pink chocolate bar into the buttercream, followed by pink metallic rods and candy pieces.

Sparkle Tart

A tart is basically a cookie (yum) with a delicious filling (double yum). That crunchy, crumbly tart shell paired with smooth, soft filling makes for the most delicious dessert. My all-time favorite filling is caramel and white chocolate ganache—which I have included in this book—however, the possibilities are endless. I once filled an entire tart shell with melted Lindt chocolate (omg!). Another time I filled one with chocolate-hazelnut spread and topped it with ice cream, cream and sprinkles. Pretty sure I was eating my emotions that day. I strongly advise against that and to just stick to this recipe.

Makes one 9-inch (23-cm) round tart

TART SHELL

½ cup (113 g) unsalted butter, cold

1½ cups (188 g) all-purpose flour

½ cup (62 g) powdered sugar

¼ tsp salt

1 large egg

½ tsp vanilla extract

Nonstick 9-inch (23-cm) tart pan

Rolling pin

Parchment paper

Pie weights or uncooked rice

1. To make the tart shell, cut the butter into cubes and set aside.

2. In a large bowl, whisk together the flour, sugar and salt.

3. Use your hands to work the butter cubes into the dry ingredients until the mixture looks like breadcrumbs.

4. Add the egg and vanilla extract and continue to mix with a fork. As soon as the dough has come together, use your hands to form a ball. Do not overwork the dough.

5. Wrap the dough in plastic wrap and press down to make a disc approximately 1 inch (2.5 cm) thick. Chill the dough in the fridge for 1 hour.

6. Spray the tart pan with nonstick cooking spray or grease it with butter or vegetable oil. Set it aside.

7. Dust a clean work surface with flour and roll out the dough until it's approximately ¼ inch (0.5 cm) thick.

8. Wrap the dough around the rolling pin and then unroll it over the tart pan.

9. With your fingertips, carefully press the pastry into all sides of the pan.

10. Trim the excess dough with a knife or roll the rolling pin over the edges of the pan. Prick the base all over with a fork and place the pan in the freezer for 30 minutes.

11. Preheat the oven to 355°F (180°C).

12. Cut a sheet of parchment paper slightly larger than the pan, crumple it up, then open it again. Remove the pan from the freezer and place the crumpled paper on top of it, then fill with pie weights or uncooked rice, spreading evenly to all sides.

13. Place the pan in the oven on the middle rack and bake for 20 minutes, then remove the paper and weights and bake for an additional 5 minutes.

14. Remove the pan from the oven and allow the tart crust to cool completely before removing it from the pan.

CARAMEL

1 (14-oz [395-g]) can sweetened condensed milk

2 tbsp (30 g) unsalted butter

2 tbsp (25 g) brown sugar

FILLINGS AND DECORATIONS

1 batch White Chocolate Ganache (page 29)

White gel food coloring

Electric/neon pink and yellow gel food coloring

Rainbow sprinkle medley

Pink sprinkle medley

Blue nonpareils

Pink and purple metallic rods

Pink pearl dragees

Silver edible stars

Rainbow confetti

Silver edible glitter

15. To make the tart's filling, start by preparing the caramel. Place all the ingredients into a medium saucepan over medium heat. Use a wooden spoon to stir continuously until the caramel thickens and begins boiling, approximately 7 minutes. Allow the caramel to cool before using it. Once the tart shell has cooled completely, pour the caramel evenly into it and chill it in the fridge for 15 minutes.

16. Make the ganache. Add 2 to 3 drops of white gel coloring and mix well to combine. Divide the ganache between two bowls and color each one individually with 2 to 3 drops of pink and yellow gel coloring.

17. Remove the tart from the fridge and pour the ganache over the caramel. Start by drizzling some of the pink ganache, followed by the yellow. Continue alternating the colors to make a marbled effect until the tart shell has been filled. Use a small offset spatula or the back of a spoon to help spread the ganache evenly. The pink and yellow ganache will blend slightly to make orange.

18. On one section of the tart, use a spoon to pour one type of sprinkles. On the section next to it, pour a different type. Continue alternating sprinkle types until the entire top of the tart is covered, then sprinkle it with glitter.

Cake Pops

What I love most about these is how they can be styled on a dessert table. Of course they taste amazing too, but unlike the cake cones, which need to remain upright so that the buttercream doesn't get squashed, these are coated with colored white chocolate that hardens. You can lay them flat on a platter or upside down on a platter or horizontally on a platter or in a pile on a platter. OK you get my drift. They also make the absolute best party favors, as they can be popped into one of those little paper bags without getting damaged. I'll take that over plastic toys and party poppers any day! Everyone will love you, especially planet Earth. Less plastic, more cake pops.

Makes 8 cake pops ···

1 batch Chocolate-Hazelnut Cupcakes (page 75)

¼ batch White Chocolate Ganache (page 29)

3 cups (510 g) white chocolate plus ½ cup (85 g) for the drizzle

8 small waffle cones

Pink, orange, yellow and purple oil-based chocolate coloring gel or powder

2 tall drinking glasses

2 piping bags

Rainbow sprinkle medley

1. Bake the chocolate-hazelnut cupcakes and set them aside to cool.

2. Once the cupcakes have completely cooled, remove them from their liners and place them in a large bowl. Use your hands to pull them apart.

3. Prepare the ganache and pour it over the crumbled cupcakes. Use your hands to mix everything together.

4. Make 8 balls approximately 3 tablespoons (75 g) each in size and place them on a cutting board lined with parchment paper. Chill them in the fridge.

5. Melt 3 cups (510 g) of the white chocolate in the microwave for 30 seconds, then in 15-second increments until it's just melted. Be careful not to overheat the chocolate, otherwise it won't set later.

6. One by one, fill each cone three-quarters full with melted chocolate. Turn the cone upside down over the bowl and twirl it until the chocolate has lined the inside and any excess has dripped out (see image on page 141). Dip the cone slightly back into the chocolate so that the rim is fully coated, then hold the cone upright. Remove a cake ball from the fridge and gently place it onto the cone. Once the chocolate around the rim of the cone sets, it will hold the ball in place. Repeat with the remaining cones and chill them in the fridge for 15 minutes. If you don't have an ice cream cone holder, then you can place the cones top down on a cutting board lined with parchment paper.

7. Reheat the remaining melted chocolate in the microwave for 15 seconds and then divide it between two bowls. Color each one individually with 2 drops of pink and orange chocolate coloring gel or a pinch of pink and orange chocolate coloring powder. Mix each one well to combine and then pour each one into the two drinking glasses.

(continued)

8. One at a time, take a cake pop from the fridge and dip it in the chocolate, making sure to coat the entire cake ball. Allow the excess chocolate to drip off before placing it down. Coat half the cake pops in the pink chocolate and the other half in the orange chocolate.

9. If you want to serve the cake pops upright, place them in a cone baking rack or holder to allow the chocolate to set. If you're serving them flat, place them directly on a sheet of parchment paper. If you're serving them upside down, place them on a sheet of parchment paper with the cone pointing up. They will be set when the chocolate is firm to touch.

10. Melt the ½ cup (85 g) of extra chocolate the same way as in step 5 and divide it between two bowls. Color each one individually with 2 drops of yellow and purple chocolate coloring gel or a pinch of yellow and purple chocolate coloring powder. Mix each one well to combine and then pour into two separate piping bags.

11. Cut the tip off the piping bag with the yellow chocolate, approximately ⅛ inch (3 mm), and drizzle it over the pink cake pops.

12. Cut the tip off the bag with the purple chocolate, approximately ⅛ inch (3 mm), and drizzle it over the orange cake pops.

13. Spoon sprinkles over the chocolate drizzle before it sets.

Cakesicles

I love things that look like one thing but are actually something else. Does that make sense? OK I'll be more specific. These little bites of heaven on a stick LOOK like ice cream pops, but they are in fact cake coated in chocolate, made in the shape of ice cream pops thanks to some pretty cool silicone molds. Revolutionary! We've certainly come a long way in the baking world. I love it because it's a great excuse to eat more cake. Some people don't want to be seen going in for a second slice of cake at parties, but a slice of cake and a cakesicle are two different things. Same, but different. It's all good. Cake in the form of something else is the future.

Makes 24 small cakesicles

1 batch Peanut Butter Cupcakes (page 74)

¼ batch White Chocolate Ganache (page 29)

3 cups (510 g) white chocolate plus ½ cup (85 g) for the drizzle

Orange, purple and green chocolate coloring gel or powder

Small silicone popsicle molds

24 small flat food-safe sticks

Piping bag

Rainbow sprinkle medley

Edible silver glitter

1. Bake the peanut butter cupcakes and set them aside to cool.

2. Once the cupcakes have completely cooled, remove them from their liners and place them in a large bowl. Use your hands to pull them apart.

3. Prepare the ganache and pour it over the crumbled cupcakes. Use your hands to mix everything together.

4. Make 24 balls approximately 1 tablespoon (25 g) each in size and place them on a cutting board covered with parchment paper. Set them aside.

5. Heat the 3 cups (510 g) of the white chocolate in the microwave for 30 seconds, then in 15-second increments until it's just melted. Be careful not to overheat the chocolate, otherwise it won't set later. Divide the chocolate between two bowls and color each one individually with 2 to 3 drops of orange and purple chocolate coloring gel or a pinch of orange and purple chocolate coloring powder. Mix each one well to combine.

6. Place the molds on a cutting board and use a spoon to drizzle chocolate into the cavities one at a time, alternating the colors. Once the bottom of the cavity is fully covered, use a spoon to coat the sides with a thick layer of melted chocolate. Insert a stick into each opening and then remove it. This will prevent any chocolate from setting over the opening and cracking the cakesicle when the sticks are inserted in the next step. Place the cutting board holding the molds into the fridge for 30 minutes to allow the chocolate to set. Do not pick up the molds directly to move them.

7. Once the chocolate has set, remove the cutting board holding the molds from the fridge. Place a ball into each cavity and push down gently, making sure there is enough room to fill the top with more melted chocolate, then insert the sticks.

8. Pour the melted chocolate into each cavity, filling them to the top. Alternate between the two colors. If the chocolate has begun to set by this point, reheat it for 15 seconds.

9. Use an offset spatula or bread knife to smooth the tops, then place the cutting board holding the molds back into the fridge to chill for 30 minutes.

(continued)

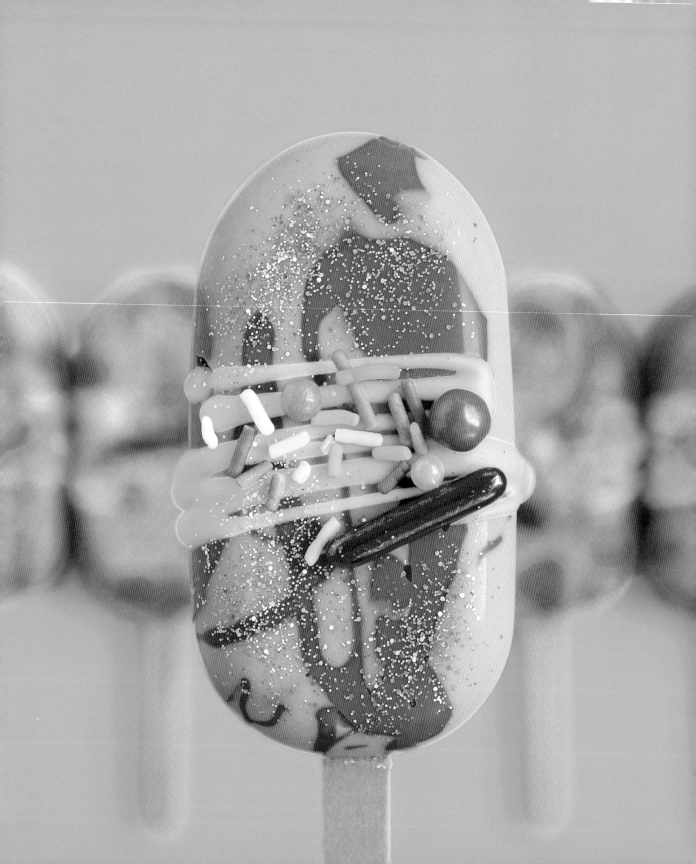

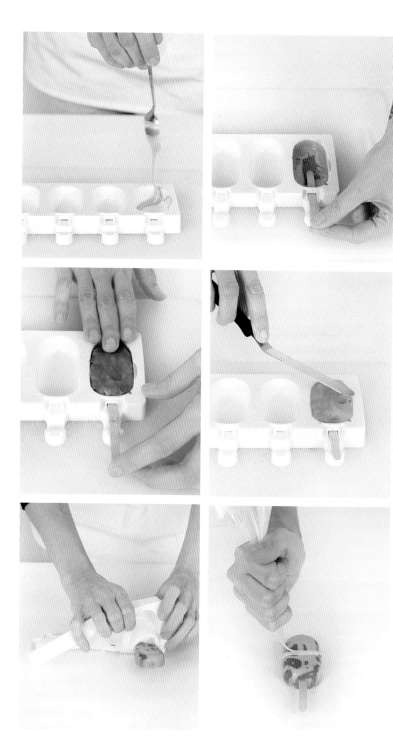

10. Gently remove the cakesicles from the molds by turning them upside down on a sheet of parchment paper and peeling the molds away.

11. Melt the ½ cup (85 g) of extra chocolate the same way as in step 5 and color it with 2 to 3 drops of green chocolate coloring gel or a pinch of green chocolate coloring powder. Mix well to combine and then pour it into the piping bag.

12. Cut the tip off the piping bag, approximately ⅛ inch (3 mm), and drizzle chocolate over the cakesicles.

13. Use a spoon to pour sprinkles over the chocolate drizzle before it sets, then glitter over the whole cakesicle.

Acknowledgments

Being a first-time author, I had no idea what to expect or how much help I'd need throughout the process of writing this book. Turns out it was a lot! Like anything difficult or demanding in life, it was made easier by the love and support of family and friends. Everyone in my life played a part along the journey, even if it was in the smallest way, like not reacting to my regular crazy outbursts or taste-testing cakes until their stomachs hurt. There are too many people to thank individually, so I'll just say thank you and I love you—you know who you are.

My beautiful children, Sebastian and Lily, you were my inspiration throughout all of this, as you are for everything I do in life. During the times when I thought I couldn't get it done and considered giving up, you both pulled me through. The best way to teach your children something is by example, and my hope is that you learned from me to work hard, never give up and always chase your dreams. This book is an amazing accomplishment for me, but you two will always be my greatest.

To the team at Page Street Publishing, in particular Rebecca Fofonoff, for giving me this amazing opportunity and believing in me. You have brought my work to life in a way that I never thought possible and I'm so grateful for that.

Finally, to my social media family: This was all possible thanks to you. Thank you for loving my work, being inspired by it and always showing me support. It is appreciated more than I'll ever be able to express. This book is for you, because of you.

About the Author

Rosie Madaschi is the creator of Sugar & Salt Cookies which was founded in 2015. As a self-taught baker, she initially baked as a hobby for friends and family. This quickly turned into a full-time career path, as she began to develop her individual style and gain popularity with her creations. This distinct style, which includes bright colors and a good eye for detail, has become easily recognizable and has inspired other bakers around the world. Her work has been featured in various online publications such as The Spruce Eats, Confetti Fair and Life's Little Celebrations. She has collaborated with Cotton On Body and charities such as Telethon and Pink Hope.

Index